LORDS OF SIPAN

A Tale of Pre-Inca Tombs, Archaeology, and Crime

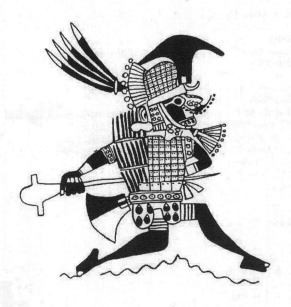

Sidney D. Kirkpatrick

Lords of Sipan, A Tale of Pre-Inca Tombs, Archaeology and Crime
© 2011 by Sidney D. Kirkpatrick
ISBN: 1466399368
ISBN-13: 9781466399365

Also by author Sidney D. Kirkpatrick:

Non-fiction:
A Cast of Killers
Turning the Tide
Edgar Cayce, An American Prophet
The Revenge of Thomas Eakins
Hitler's Holy Relics

All the pen and ink illustrations that appear throughout this book are taken from original Moche designs and motifs found in the Moche Archive at UCLA, courtesy of Donna McClelland and Christopher Donnan. Paintings of the archaeological finds at Huaca Rajada are courtesy of Ned M. Seidler and Tom Hall. The photographs of archaeological personnel and artifacts are courtesy of Walter Alva and Guillermo Cock.

"I'm often asked how a man can live his entire life excavating under the hot sun in the parched desert sands. But that's its main attraction. Because the same hot sun and parched sand that protects the monuments of the past also preserves their makers."

—Walter Alva

This book is dedicated to Andean scholar Guillermo Cock

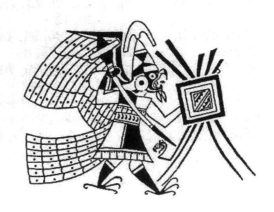

Contents

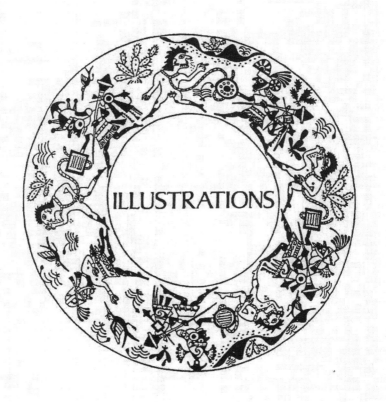

ILLUSTRATIONS

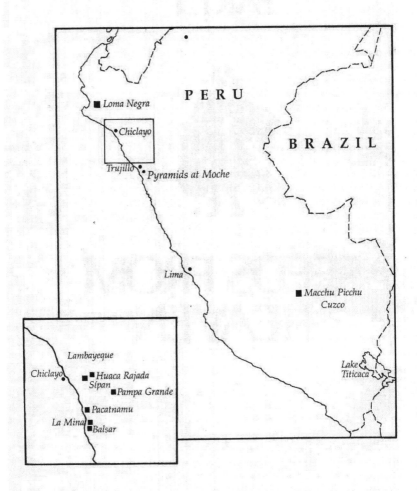

Map of Peru with insert showing primary locations of archaeological finds.

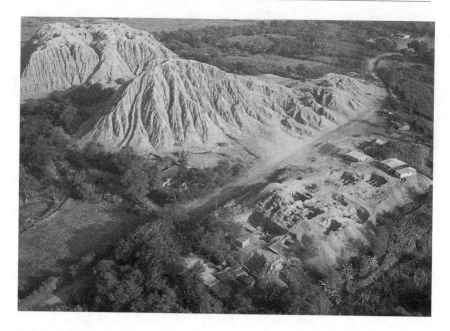

Arial view of the Huaca Rajada archaeological site at Sipan. The two "hills" (center and upper left) are actually pre-Columbian pyramids whose adobe brick coverings have been washed away by centuries of El Nino rains. Excavation is underway at the third smaller pyramid where the discoveries were made.

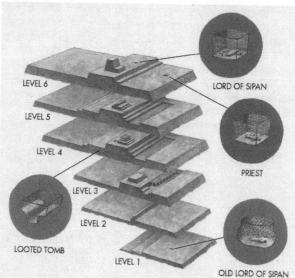

The illustration above shows the layers of ancient construction and burial chambers unearthed at Huaca Rajada. With each new burial another layer of bricks was added.

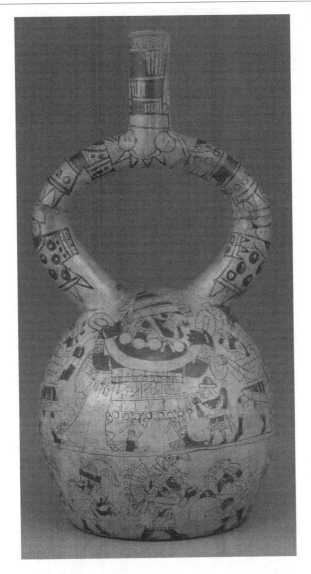

Moche "stirrup-spout" ceramic displaying a fine-line drawing of a Moche Lord and ceremonial figures wearing distinctive helmets, jewelry, weapons and instruments.

Next: an artist's illustration of the Lord of Sipan's burial possessions excavated at Huaca Rajada.

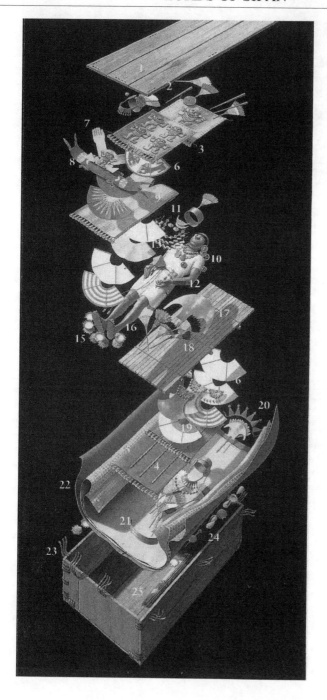

Beneath the coffin's three planked lid: (1) feather ornaments, (2) both above and below the body. Fabric banners with gilded copper platelets depicting a figure with turquoise-bead bracelets lay face up above the body (3) and facedown below. (4) Copper struts (5) made the lower banners rigid. Eleven chest coverings, called pectorals, of shell and copper beads (6) also appear in layers. A gilded copper headdress (7) lay atop a textile headband to secure it. (8) An outer shirt covered with gilded copper platelets and cone shaped tassels at the hem (9) and a simple inner white garment (10) clothed the body. The skull, face, ears, neck and chest were festooned with gold silver and copper ornaments (11) Turquoise and gold-bead bracelets adorned the forearms (12) Gold and copper ingots lay on his hands; the right held a gold rattle (13) the left a copper knife. (14) Seashells (15) lay at the his feet, clad in ceremonial copper sandals (16). Beneath the ruler a massive gold headdress ornament (17) overlays a wood support frame (18) Under it were crescent-shaped gold bells, two attached to back-flaps of gold and copper. (19) A small gold headdress ornament was found near a copper headdress, chin strap (20) The significance of copper strips (21) remains a mystery. Three shrouds, two sewn with gilded copper platelets (22) enfolded the contents of the coffin, fastened together with copper strapping (23). At the very bottom lay shells, a miniature war club and shield (24), and copper-pointed hunting darts (25).

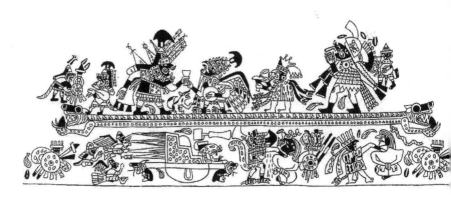

Above: Fine-line drawing from a stirrup-spout ceramic depicting a Moche lord participating in a sacrificial ceremony as believed to have taken place atop the Huaca Rajada pyramid.

Next: important figures of the sacrificial ceremony as depicted in fine-line drawing on Moche ceramic.

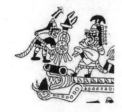

Anthropomorphized animal warrior (upper left), standing on a serpent and holding a weapons bundle with club and shield.

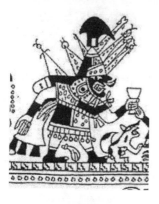

Moche lord, recognized by the rays emanating from his head. His size is large relative to the other figures in the scene, and he is being presented with a goblet by a figure holding a disk. He consistently wears a conical helmet with a crescent-shaped ornament at its peak, a back-flap, and a short shirt and skirt.

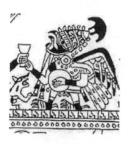

High Priest. He holds a disk in one hand and a goblet in the other. He normally is shown presenting the goblet to the lord. He is always part bird and part human, and wears either a conical helmet or a headdress.

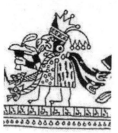

High Priestess. She holds a goblet in one hand and appears to be covering it with a gourd plate that is held in the other. Her clothes include a long shirt and a headdress with tassel ornaments in front and behind.

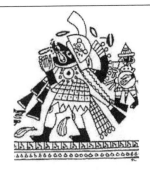

High Priest or Lesser Lord. This figure can be recognized from certain details of clothing, primarily the streamers with serrated upper edges that hang from his shoulders and the other sash-like object with a series of disks at the border. The figure also wears an elaborate nose ornament and a characteristic headdress.

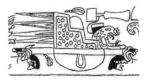

Throne or litter. Note the attached rattle with the cutting blade on the upper right corner.

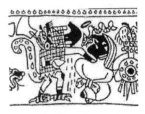

An anthropomorphized feline warrior in the process of drawing blood from a bound, nude prisoner.

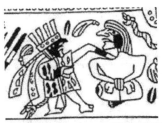

A human figure in the process of drawing blood from a bound nude prisoner. Note (lower right), a variety of papaya known as an ulluchu fruit which may have been used as an anticoagulant.

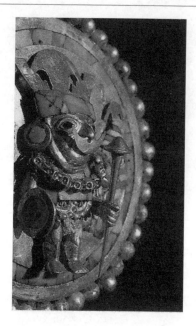

Above: Gold and turquoise ear ornament from the tomb of the Lord of Sipan.

Below: Tunnels that looters carved into the pyramid platform.

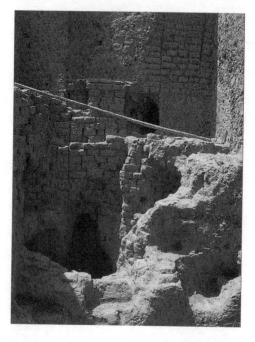

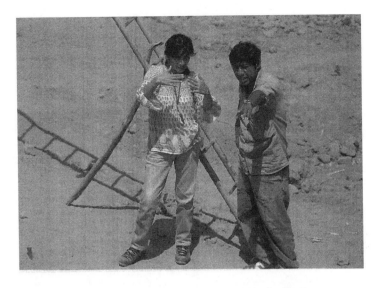

Above: Archaeologists Susan Alva and Luis Chero Zurita

Below: Dr. Walter Alva

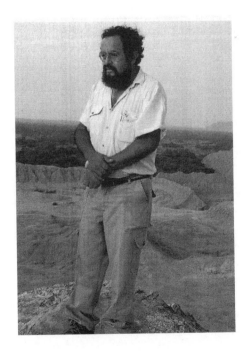

The main platform of the looted pyramid after excavation has begun.

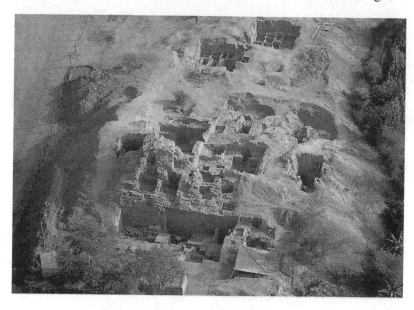

Archaeologists removing the Lord of Sipan's bones

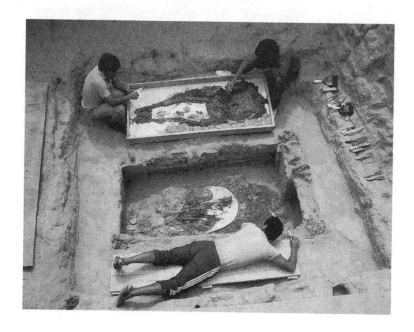

Jaguar head looted by Ernil Bernal and his men

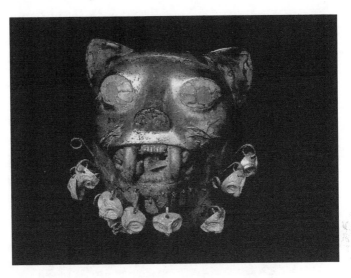

Miniature Moche Lord looted by Ernil Bernal and his men

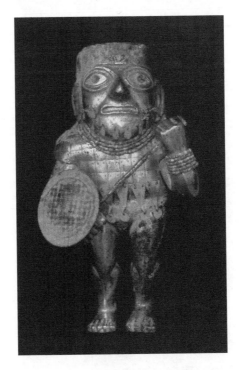

Antiquities smuggler David Swetnam holding a looted gold peanut bead.

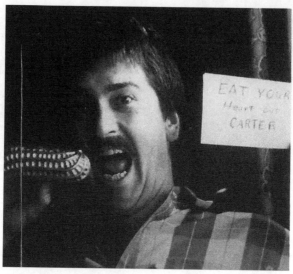

U.S. Customs Agent Gaston Wallace

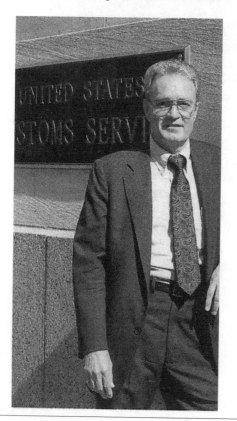

The Lord of Sipan's headdress and back-flap with moon-shaped rattles

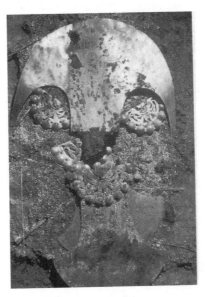

Below: The cache of ceramics found adjacent to the Lord of Sipan's tomb.

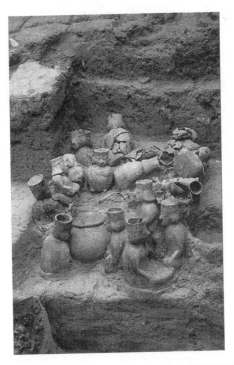

Below: the skull of the Lord of Sipan with necklace of moon-shaped discs.

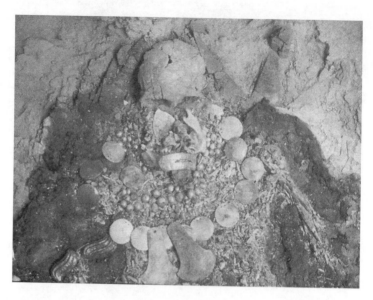

Upper layer of burial possessions of the Old Lord of Sipan

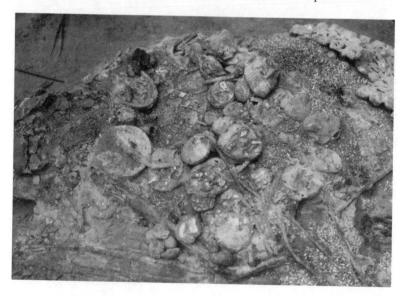

Below: Removing the bones of the Old Lord of Sipan

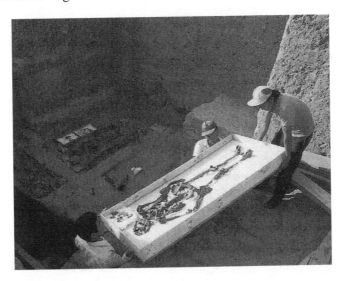

Author Sidney D. Kirkpatrick (left) with Susan Alva (right) and archaeologists at the Sipan excavation.

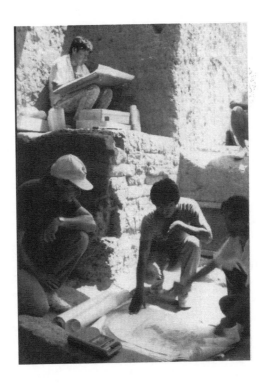

PART 1

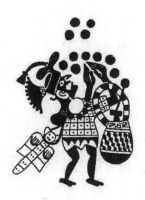

SEEDS FROM HEAVEN

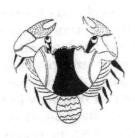

1

For more than a millennium, tons of temple brick and loose rock preserved the royal tombs of an ancient, pre-Inca civilization known as the Moche, a culture that flourished in the coastal valleys of northern Peru at the same time that Rome ruled the Mediterranean world. The location of the Moche tombs, in the heart of Huaca Rajada, a pyramid complex on the remote, sunbaked, coastal plains of Lambayeque, remained a lost secret until a team of ten impoverished thieves penetrated one of the tombs on a cool, moonlit night in February 1987. Numerous accounts exist of how this tomb came to be opened, but none is more accurate or compelling than those of the looters themselves.

Thirty-six-year-old Ernil Bernal, an unemployed truck mechanic and the self-appointed spokesman for the tomb looters, took immense pleasure in recounting the events to friends and neighbors at the local cantina in Sipan, a small village of mud and cinder-block cottages less than a mile from the pyramid he desecrated. A handsome young man with jet-black hair, a loose smile, and large, expressive hands, Ernil embellished his story with the passage of time; but police investigators have corroborated the important points, and Ernil's teammates are in complete accord about what happened on the night they ransacked the first tomb.

At ten-thirty P.M. on February 6, Ernil crawled on his hands and knees into the toe of a twenty-three-foot boot-shaped tunnel which he and his men had carved into the northwest face of the smallest of the three large pyramids that compose Huaca Rajada. Less than a quarter of the size of the two pyramids beside it, this structure rose only sixty feet from its wide rectangular base to its square, flat-topped pinnacle. Access to the tunnel was a path leading from an unpaved road that separated the pyramid from the other two. A tent of thick vines and eucalyptus trees afforded adequate cover should one of the infrequent police patrols come too close, or a farmer from the surrounding sugarcane field notice the telltale heap of backfill that the looters deposited on the sloping steps leading to the top of the platform.

Inside the looters' tunnel, Ernil heaved his pick and shovel aside and ran a practiced hand over the hardened adobe bricks that lined the ceiling. Moving his fingertips sideways six or seven inches at a time, he inspected the uppermost portion of the ceiling for imperfections in the pitted and coarse surface until his right index finger settled on a peanut-shaped lump in the clay mortar between two bricks. His back arched, his knees jammed into the sidewalls for support, he found it next to impossible to take a close look at the dark mass of the ceiling above him. But even with his eyes closed, he knew he had discovered something far more valuable than a pair of loose pebbles pressed together between two bricks. Experience had taught him that these were carved beads: the first on what would be a long strand that the pyramid builders, more than a thousand years earlier, had tossed into the wet mortar to please the ancestral spirits. Because of their ancient origin, looters called these beads "seeds from heaven."

Ernil snapped his thumb and index finger closed and plucked the first bead from between the two bricks. Before he had the bead securely in his palm, he plucked out a second bead, then probed again, this time running his fingernails into the groove between the two bricks, picking out a third bead, and yet another, until he had as many as he could hold in one hand. Turning his shoulders sideways, he began to probe with his left hand. When this hand was also full, he dropped into a crouch beside his kerosene lantern to examine what he had found.

Eight hammered gold beads. Ninety percent pure. Ernil knew this the moment he weighed them in his palm, then rolled the beads back and forth between his fingers to remove the thin crust of dried mortar that had sealed the beads between the bricks. He could see how brightly they shone in the light from his lantern.

His reaction was not so much joy as relief, for he himself had proposed coming to Huaca Rajada instead of prospecting at a nearby cemetery, where he and his men could be assured of obtaining a gold wedding ring or pocket watch. Ernil and the others had been carving tunnels into the Huaca Rajada pyramids in two-hour shifts since the middle of November the year before, and during those three months of agonizing labor in hot, mosquito-infested tunnels, they had unearthed nothing besides ceramic pots and piles of animal bones. And the clay bricks that composed Huaca Rajada repelled the advances he made upon them, becoming harder and more resistant to his pick and shovel than any he had encountered before. His muscles ached. A callus on his hand had begun again to blister.

Like his wife, Esmilda, and his friend Chalo, Ernil's partners had begun to lose confidence in him. Half of the original team of *huaqueros*, or tomb looters, had abandoned the site because nothing of importance had been found; others hadn't returned because they had caught chills from spending too many hours in the narrow and cramped tunnels; still another had fled the site for fear that ancestral spirits would seek retribution upon him for defiling their sacred monument. Ernil knew better than to believe the local superstitions. Nor had he any fear of the cramped and narrow crawlspaces.

Ernil's concern was police intervention, which was why he had threatened Mercedes Zapata, a toothless old woman who lived in a thatched-roof hovel at the foot of the pyramid. For the time being, he could assure her silence; not so that of her son, thirty-six-year-old Ricardo. Because of his mother's proximity to the site, Ricardo considered Huaca Rajada his personal property and resented Ernil's intrusion. A nonverbal threat, in the form of a pistol applied to Ricardo's temple, had been required to keep him from turning to police authorities.

Fear of police intervention had also been the reason why Ernil parked his blue Toyota pickup truck out of sight from the main road, why he and his men slept during the daylight hours and worked only at night, and why Ernil posted at least one man with a pistol in a strategic position overlooking the road leading from police headquarters in Chiclayo. No one could come or go from Huaca Rajada without the knowledge of Ernil or one of his men.

A hundred or more hours spent carving tunnels into Huaca Rajada had now reaped a rich reward. Ernil could get as much as seventeen dollars for each of his gold beads on the black market, and as much as twenty if he found enough to make an entire necklace that he could sell to one of the important antiquities dealers in Trujillo or Lima. Then he could pay the other men for the time they had spent underground, plus a huge bonus to himself, and still have a bead left over to give to his mother as a lucky charm.

Ernil deposited the beads in a cloth sack around his waist and raised his lantern to inspect the tunnel ceiling. He noticed a strange discoloration in the bricks above him, as though the builders had run out of one type of clay and switched to another, or made a structural mistake that required a patch to be placed over the bricks. He had never seen a construction technique like this in all the years he had been hunting for treasure inside pyramids. But nothing about Huaca Rajada made much sense to him. At each excavated level, the architecture of the pyramid changed. His men had uncovered European burials, Inca mummies, chambers full of animal and human bones, and large, carved stone boulders of unknown origin.

The size and shape of the bricks surrounding the patch in the ceiling above him indicated that the section of the pyramid he had tunneled into had been built by the Moche, a civilization not generally associated with Huaca Rajada.

For a moment, Ernil considered calling Chalo or the other men for advice or help. Instead, he set his lantern down on the tunnel floor, wiped the sweat off his bare arms and chest, and reached into his tool sack for a four-foot iron rod, the kind he used to probe cemeteries for unmarked graves. Holding the handle of the T-shaped rod tightly in his hands, he drove it upward as hard as he could into the tunnel ceiling. But instead of striking rock-hard clay bricks as he expected, the iron rod slid smoothly up to its hilt, as if sucked inside, throwing Ernil off balance and onto his knees. As he looked up through the swirl of dust rising off the tunnel floor, he could see a fine, dry white sand pouring in a trickling stream out of the opening he had made with the iron rod.

Mesmerized by the trickle, Ernil remained where he had fallen, never realizing that for each second he lingered inside the tunnel, an ever-increasing amount of sand poured through the hole. Soon the stream became a river and the river became a torrent, and Ernil was buried under a shower of loose pyramid brick and fallen earth.

Huaqueros had perished in cave-ins for as long as there had been *huacas*, or sacred sites, to tunnel into. Huaca Rajada was no exception. Ernil knew this because he had been raised in the shadow of Huaca Rajada's mountains of clay brick at his father's small farmhouse, and had heard the stories about the "hungry huacas" from his mother and his uncle. In the most lurid of these stories, larger-than-life bats, owls, and cats accosted villagers and carried them to the pyramids for sacrifice to ancestral spirits buried in hidden chambers deep inside the ancient monuments. Killer dogs howled at the moon in another story. Teenagers, lured to one of the pyramids by the heavenly sound of panpipes, lost fingers, toes, and other body parts to creatures that had human legs and animal heads. Ernil himself had helped spread these stories in order to scare the superstitious villagers into staying away from the site, leaving the pyramids for him to plunder.

Trapped inside the tunnel at Huaca Rajada, panic setting in, Ernil started to wonder if the stories were true: that ancestral spirits had lured him into the pyramid, and that in a matter of moments the same spirits would remove body parts for sacrifice, or killer dogs would descend upon him. Ernil cursed his negligence for having scaled the pyramid steps before furnishing the spirits with a *pago*, or payment, in the form of liquor, food, and tobacco, a precaution huaqueros had taken for centuries. He told himself that he should have listened to his older brother Emilio's advice and stayed at his uncle's jungle farm and earned a decent living repairing trucks used to haul coca leaves to private airstrips. But he had grown lonely without his wife and two children, and his father had become ill, suffering from meningitis. Like six of his eight brothers, Ernil had returned to his childhood home and become a huaquero.

Ernil lay pinned where he had fallen, listening to the earth settle around him and thinking each moment would be his last. Just as he had given up hope of ever seeing daylight again, he heard the scraping of picks and shovels as his teammates cleared a passage toward him through the debris. Ernil's brother Emilio and his friend Chalo called out to him. Ernil summoned his strength to answer. He craned his neck as the first shafts from their lanterns broke the darkness.

Inexplicably, the men stood their distance, peering into the tunnel at him as if they feared that they would meet the same end as Ernil should they take one step closer.

Ernil realized the error he had made as he called out to his teammates a second time. He had mistaken his brother's astonishment for fear. Ernil's iron rod had punctured the floor of a room suspended above his tunnel: a hidden chamber inside Huaca Rajada that had gone unnoticed until its contents poured onto Ernil like an avalanche.

In the light from his brother's lantern, Ernil could see that he had been buried up to his shoulders in a treasure-trove of priceless gold and silver ornaments, ancient carvings studded with precious stones, and bones so old that he could literally see them disintegrate as the cold night air filled the once-secret mausoleum.

In the hours ahead, Ernil and his men would work at a feverish pace to remove from the burial chamber giant gold masks, foot-long knives of gold and silver, thick chains of peanut-shaped beads, and molded figurines of crabs, cats, jaguars, horned monsters, and a curious little man holding an equally curious shield and what looked like an oversized rattle. By sunrise the original tunnel had tripled in size as Ernil and his men probed for hidden compartments. By three o'clock that following afternoon, more than six new tunnels catacombed the pyramid's interior. Teams of other huaqueros had begun to descend upon Huaca Rajada like flies to honey.

Haggard and exhausted, Ernil's men emerged carrying a total of eleven rice sacks filled with treasure—enough, by one huaquero's estimate, to "turn the poorest man among them into the richest hacienda owner on the coastal plains."

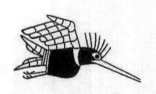

2

Chance led the thieves to a treasure beyond their expectations, and avarice soon took it from them. Tomb looter would turn on tomb looter for a larger share of the plunder. Heated arguments resulted in a shoot-out. Blood would splatter the huaqueros' tunnels. No two accounts of the shooting are the same; but it is clear that Ernil and his brothers claimed nine out of the eleven sacks of plundered loot, that one of the original ten huaqueros was killed by three shots in the chest, and that another huaquero escaped across the sugarcane fields and called the police.

The one man destined to play the most important role in the later excavation and protection of Huaca Rajada was then contacted by investigators. Known to the police and the huaqueros alike for his tireless decade-long campaign to protect the ancient monuments under his management, Dr. Walter Alva, inspector general of archaeology in Lambayeque for the National Institute of Culture, or INC, had the expertise and knowledge to track the movements and sale of Huaca Rajada's looted antiquities on the local black market. The thirty-five-year-old Alva had also earned the respect and admiration of scholars at home and abroad as director of the Bruning Museum, a once second-rate, poorly organized regional museum that he had transformed into a small but impressive showcase for the cultures of the coastal plains.

Local police did not contact Alva at the Bruning Museum in the city of Lambayeque until just before midnight on Wednesday, February 25, 1987, more than two weeks after Ernil and his men had plundered their first tomb at Huaca Rajada. At the time of the call, Alva was sound asleep in his modest two-bedroom home in the rear courtyard. The night patrolman, sent to waken Alva, told him that the chief of police of Lambayeque was requesting that he come to police headquarters in Chiclayo to examine a sack of plundered artifacts that investigators had seized in the home of a local huaquero.

The good-natured Alva masked his surprise at being roused out of bed for something short of a terrorist plot to steal his prized showcase of pre-Inca gold ornaments in the museum's vault. Like the rest of the Bruning staff, the night patrolman knew that he had been in bed for three days fighting a severe case of bronchitis, and that Alva's wife, Susana, had left strict orders that her husband not be disturbed while she was away visiting her mother in Trujillo.

When Alva picked up the receiver on the night patrolman's desk and introduced himself, the message already given the night patrolman was repeated: The Peruvian Investigative Police, or PIP, in the nearby city of Chiclayo had uncovered a looting operation at a local pyramid, raided the home of the alleged leader, brought in two suspects for questioning, and seized a rice sack full of plundered artifacts. Walter Mondragon, the departmental chief of police of Lambayeque, had issued orders that Alva, in his joint capacity as inspector general of archaeology and director of the Bruning Museum, present himself at police headquarters to examine the seized items at once.

As Alva well knew, huaqueros are stopped and questioned by police in Peru almost as routinely as prostitutes or common thieves. And in the five-thousand-square-mile Department of Lambayeque, an area that includes more than ten thousand archaeological sites, huaqueros had practiced their profession for as long as brothels had operated in the red-light districts and teams of pickpockets had roamed the markets. But never before had Mondragon summoned Alva out of bed in the middle of the night and requested that he make the thirty-five-minute drive along the wind-swept Pan-American highway to Chiclayo, the capital of Lambayeque, to examine plundered artifacts.

"What we have here," Assistant Police Chief Edmundo Temoche, Mondragon's next in command, told Alva, "is sure to make your fever go away."

Alva was skeptical, but agreed to come because he counted on Mondragon's continued support for the work at the museum, just as Mondragon counted on Alva's expertise at police headquarters, an arrangement that had begun when Alva had assumed his first post as assistant director of the Bruning and Mondragon had been appointed chief of police of the city of Chiclayo. At that time, the summer of 1978, Mondragon had asked Alva for help investigating reports that a mass murderer was stalking the city streets in Chiclayo and leaving his dismembered victims to rot on a beach in Eten, a small seaside village fifteen miles to the south. Since Mondragon hadn't been able to locate a coroner, he did the next best thing: He sent for Alva, who knew about bones from the physical anthropology courses that were required of all student archaeologists at the University of Trujillo. To

Mondragon's surprise, Alva immediately cracked the case wide open when he identified the human remains as pre-Hispanic bones that had come out of the two-thousand-year-old Eten cemetery. Local children had dug the bones out of the ground and made arrangements of them on the beach.

As their relationship grew, Alva and Mondragon discovered in one another a shared belief that it was their duty to preserve Peru's cultural heritage, something that many of their colleagues deemed relatively unimportant in a region that had more than its share of poverty, malaria, terrorism, inflation, and corruption. They also realized how their respective skills complemented one another. Mondragon knew how to run an investigation, but had little real understanding of the special archaeological significance of the area he had been assigned to police. Alva knew the area's archaeological past, but had been unable to prevent the wholesale looting of its archaeological sites by huaqueros.

Minutes after he hung up the phone, Alva, dressed in a pair of khaki pants and a short-sleeved shirt, sat in the passenger seat of a brand-new Volkswagen van, a recent gift from the museum's chief benefactor, the Federal Republic of Germany. Benedicto, the museum's driver, handyman, and chief trouble-shooter, pulled out onto the deserted streets of Lambayeque, past the sixteenth-century cathedral of Saint Peter, and onto the Pan-American highway. From here, the city quickly disappeared, and all that could be seen were one rice or sugarcane field after another and an occasional strip of sand where the irrigation ditches stopped. The road, such as it was, followed the packed sand that bordered the fields, as flat and straight as the fields themselves, broken only by a stranded bus or derelict truck pushed into one of the drainage ditches.

Except for these lush green fields, all of them within the confines of six major irrigated valleys, the north coast of Peru was sheer desert where nothing grew, nothing decayed, and the only structures to break the horizon were giant pyramids.

As he had on previous missions to speak to the PIP about huaqueros, Alva couldn't help but wonder which of the many archaeological sites under his jurisdiction had been sacked of its treasures this time. The barren terrain on either side of the road bore hundreds of thousands of pockmarks where huaqueros, armed with steel rods, picks, shovels, and kerosene lamps, had probed for burials. And virtually all the looting at these sites had taken place in the last five years, long after the government of Peru had proclaimed blanket ownership of all cultural property, prohibited its export, and made looting of archaeological sites a criminal offense.

More often than not, the huaqueros committing these offenses left nothing behind for scholars to study but scattered bones and scraps of rotting textiles. Their loot, frequently a single ceramic vase or metal ornament, almost always disappeared into an insatiable international black market for stolen pre-Hispanic treasures. As a consequence, what awaited him at police headquarters, Alva was sure, would be but the poorest castoffs of a poor thief.

Mondragon's men met Alva in front of the police station on the main boulevard in Chiclayo. Normally, the van would have been searched as a precaution against terrorists; but Mondragon had notified his men ahead of time, and Alva was immediately ushered to the central dispatch desk, where he signed in. An officer wearing a webbed gun belt and military fatigues escorted him down the hall to the second room on the left, Mondragon's outer office.

Alva had been inside Mondragon's office many times before, so he knew what to expect. An overstuffed sofa sat against the side wall. A pair of chairs were under the window directly in front of the door, and a small desk was on the right, with a large framed photograph of Alan Garcia, the president of the Republic of Peru, hanging above it. This picture covered a hole in the plaster where terrorists had once fired a bullet intended to kill Mondragon. A jovial, good-humored man in his late fifties, the police chief took great pleasure in showing the bullet hole to visitors as confirmation that he was born under a lucky star.

To Alva's surprise, the sofa in Mondragon's office was occupied by a child, a young girl no older than Alva's own seven-year-old son Bruno, at that moment with his mother and older brother, Nacho, in Trujillo. Beside the girl was an old woman with gray hair who, Alva later learned, was Eloisa Bernal, Ernil Bernal's mother and grandmother to the young girl, Rebecca Bernal, one of Ernil's two daughters.

Dressed as usual in a pressed shirt and starched trousers, Mondragon stood on the opposite side of the room. A large, muscular, imposing figure with a black pencil-thin mustache, he would have been taken for a police officer whether or not he was wearing his uniform. Alva, by contrast, was small and robust with bushy eyebrows and a thick beard, and he wouldn't be mistaken for a policeman even if he were in uniform.

As Alva came inside, Mondragon held out a gold bead that he had removed from around the neck of the old woman. Large numbers of these beads, Mondragon explained, had recently flooded the black market in Chiclayo. A local jeweler had contacted the police to tell them that he had received a dozen or more requests to melt similar beads into ingots. In response, Mondragon and the PIP launched an investigation to track the beads back to their source, a small cantina in the village of Sipan, about an hour's drive from Chiclayo.

Alva was not impressed. Beads like the one in Mondragon's hand often turned up on the black market in Chiclayo or, farther south, in Trujillo. Apparently someone had unearthed a long strand and begun to use the beads instead of cash. Moreover, the two so-called huaqueros sitting on the sofa didn't look as if they could dig a drainage ditch, let alone plunder a pre-Hispanic tomb. Mondragon, to Alva's way of thinking, would be better off making a formal apology and letting his "suspects" return home.

Mondragon assured Alva that he had told him only part of the story. While one team of investigators was tracking the source of the gold beads to the Sipan cantina, a local huaquero contacted police headquarters and told them that Ernil Bernal, his brothers, and his associates had plundered a Moche tomb at Huaca Rajada overflowing with ancient treasures, and that the gold beads appearing on the black market represented little more than souvenirs Ernil and his associates were handing out for tips. Another police informant, Mrs. Mercedes Zapata, described as a year-round resident of Huaca Rajada, confirmed the report, claiming that Ernil and his men had threatened her to keep quiet. Mondragon had raided the Bernal house, seized a rice sack of loot hidden in a sideboard in the kitchen, and arrested Eloisa Bernal because she was the only suspect present. Ernil's daughter Rebecca had come along because there was no one else in the house to look after her.

Mondragon's report puzzled Alva, leading him to suspect that the chief of police or one of his men had been the target of an elaborate hoax. After all, Huaca Rajada was not commonly associated with the Moche but with the

Chimu, a later pre-Inca culture that had once made its home in the same area. Alva and his assistant archaeologist had confirmed this during a preliminary examination of the site less than a year earlier on a routine trip to visit other sites in the immediate vicinity. And even if Alva had made a mistake, an unwritten code of behavior governed the looting of tombs. Huaqueros never turned to the police, especially in Sipan, a backward settlement of twenty or thirty primitive homes that had no toilets and no running water. Most had no doors. People here settled their own differences, as they had for hundreds of years.

Ernil Bernal's name, on the other hand, piqued Alva's curiosity because he was descended from a long line of huaqueros alleged to have organized looting operations throughout the Department of Lambayeque. Family members had also been implicated in auto theft, illegal narcotics sales, and murder. Their family farmhouse on the outskirts of Sipan was less than a ten-minute walk to the Huaca Rajada pyramids.

Before Alva could ask what proof investigators had obtained from the Bernal house, Mondragon signaled for Assistant Police Chief Temoche, the senior officer in charge of the investigation, to show the suspects out of the room. After they had left, Mondragon walked over to the desk, picked up a package wrapped in brown paper, and handed it to Alva.

Alva judged the package to be about three and a half pounds, about the shape and size of a cantaloupe. Based on his experience, he guessed it to be a ceramic pot with some unusual designs or insignia that had caught Mondragon's attention and convinced him that the piece was valuable.

Never had Alva been more mistaken. Inside was an intricately crafted human head made of hammered sheet gold, with eyes of silver and cobalt pupils of rare lapis lazuli, too perfect to have been a clever forgery, and clearly not an artifact that a looter came upon more than once in a lifetime, if at all.

Huaqueros had managed to loot something worth a king's ransom, and the quality and style told Alva that the piece did indeed belong to the Moche civilization, that he must have been mistaken about the origins and purpose of the pyramid complex of Huaca Rajada. No Peruvian artifact as significant as this had ever reached the hands of an archaeologist.

Mondragon had more to show him. A second package contained the golden head of a puma, baring teeth of pearl-white polished seashells and golden eyes in the shape of teardrops. This piece was also plainly made by Moche artisans, a priceless companion to the death mask and clearly out of the same collection.

Next, Mondragon handed Alva handfuls of shiny gold beads and an assortment of nose rings made of hammered gold and silver shaped to form crescent moons. In still another package, a pair of gold and silver peanuts gleamed three times natural size, wrinkled and ridged precisely like real peanuts. But it was the last package that captured Alva's greatest interest, for it contained an eight-inch ceremonial gold rattle in the shape of a half-moon. Incised upon it was indisputable confirmation of the origin of the artifacts: the carved figure of a fearsome Moche deity holding a ceremonial knife in one hand and the decapitated head of a prisoner in the other.

Alva was left speechless. If what he saw before him was to be believed, huaqueros had discovered something that most archaeologists doubted the existence of and that treasure hunters had spent centuries searching for but never found: the long-lost tomb of a Moche lord.

3

Less than a month earlier, Alva had lectured a class of visiting schoolchildren on the mysteries of the Moche civilization. In the course of his lecture, Alva had spoken of his lifelong fascination with the Moche culture and espoused a theory that most archaeologists and scholars rejected as fanciful: the existence of a royal Moche tomb, comparable in riches and splendor to the tomb of an ancient Egyptian pharaoh. Now that Alva had tangible evidence that such a tomb had been unearthed, his lecture held a special relevance far beyond the scope of his activities as a regional archaeologist for the INC or as the young director of a small coastal-plains museum.

For Alva, the first step toward any understanding of the Moche civilization lay in an appreciation of how little scholars knew about its culture. In spite of the existence of hundreds of Moche burial sites, and evidence of vast pyramid and ceremonial complexes, ruined cities, and exquisite examples of ceramic art, researchers could not authenticate any Moche religious practices; nor could they isolate one important event in the Moche's eight-hundred-year history, or put a name to a single Moche poet, musician, architect, priest, soldier, or ruler. The kingdom of the Moche, Alva had told the schoolchildren, was "the land of the unknown dead."

Early histories of Peru, written primarily by Spanish missionaries and chroniclers who accompanied Pizarro and the conquistadors on their conquest of the Inca Empire in 1533, never even included the Moche. To these invaders, Peru was little more than a source of gold and souls to be saved. Once these tasks were speedily accomplished, the natives became a source of cheap labor in mines, fields, and textile mills. But Pizarro and his conquistadors may not have been the first to plunder the Peruvian temples and burial sites or to pass judgment on its history. Evidence exists that the Incas plundered many of their predecessors' temples and burial sites while their historians censored much of the known past to validate their own version of historical events. Moche pyramids became a source of accessible building sites for their conquerors just as the remains of the Roman Empire became quarries for the Renaissance man. Tomb looting became a tradition in Peru passed on from one generation to the next, similar to practices in Egypt.

Taking the lead from Pizarro, European treasure hunters and missionaries exhausted the more obvious sources of gold from the Inca temples and turned their attention to plundering the enormous north-coast monuments. Prospecting licenses were granted, corporations formed, stock issued, and contemporary mining techniques employed to tunnel inside the pyramids. In the best known and most notorious case, treasure hunters diverted a leg of a river in the Moche Valley to flood the base of a pyramid complex and lay its contents bare. As more treasure hunters arrived, maps to the important sites were sold along with the tools necessary to loot them. At that time, pre-Columbian art, meaning any art manufactured before Christopher Columbus arrived in the Americas in 1492, held practically no value besides its weight in precious metals.

Thus, later researchers and historians had little besides scant archaeological evidence with which to study Peru's earliest cultures. In 1896, Max Uhle, a brilliant and eccentric German archaeologist, began the first scientific excavation intended to reveal more about the past rather than to enrich museum collections. The spectacular discovery in 1911 by Hiram Bingham of the forgotten city of Machu Picchu triggered popular interest in the ancient civilizations, as did breakthroughs by Julio Tello, the father of Peruvian archaeology. Even so, the older pre-Inca cultures remained an enigma. Not until 1937, with the founding of the Institute of Andean Research and its later excavations at the Viru Valley, did research into the Moche culture take an important step forward.

Prior to the Viru Valley excavations, most researchers and historians lumped all the pre-Inca cultures on the north coast together, calling them Chimu, or proto-Chimu. Archaeologists excavating in the Viru Valley in 1946, however, chose to use the term Mochica, later simplified to Moche, a word they derived from the name of the north-coast river valley presumed to have been the birthplace of the Moche civilization. For the first time since archaeologists had come to Peru, Viru Valley excavators published photographs and an accompanying report of a tomb that belonged to a high-ranking Moche priest and his retainers.

Breakthroughs in Moche research were also made by Rafael Larco Herrera, a self-taught native-born archaeologist who amassed a collection of more than ten thousand Moche ceramics at his sprawling north-coast sugar hacienda. His son, Rafael Larco Hoyle, greatly enlarged his father's program of excavation and collection and published the first scientific books devoted solely to the culture of the Moche. Later came scholars and archaeologists such as Gerdt Kutscher, Richard Schaedel, Elizabeth Benson, Donna McClelland, Michael Moseley, and Izumi Shimada. Foremost among these new Moche scholars was Christopher B. Donnan, the young professor of anthropology and director of the Fowler Museum of Cultural History at the University of California at Los Angeles, whose books, *Moche Art of Peru* and *Ancient Burial Patterns of the Moche Valley*, quickly became the accepted texts for Moche research, earning him an undisputed reputation as the international authority on Moche culture and civilization.

But in spite of the inroads these scholars made, all that could be said with any certainty about the Moche was that their culture existed on the north coast somewhere between 100 B.C. and A.D. 700, soon after the fall of a civilization known as the Chavin and before the rise of a civilization known as the Chimu.

Like the Egyptians, the Moche lived in one of the largest and driest deserts in the world, stretching from Lambayeque in the north to Nepena in the south, a distance of more than four hundred miles. Their settlements were confined to the six major river valleys on the north coast that drained rainfall from the mountains back to the sea, a region about sixty miles from east to west. During the middle and late years of Moche occupation, a period archaeologists refer to as Moche III and Moche IV, each of the north-coast valleys contained at least one sizable monument built by that culture. Trading and commerce, however, must have taken place even beyond these boundaries as evidenced by the Moche's access to precious stones such as lapis lazuli, mined hundreds of miles to the south of known Moche occupation. To the north of their known occupation, traders obtained spondylus shells, conch, mother-of-pearl, and other seashells for ornaments. Moche explorers must have also traveled hundreds of miles east, into the tropical rain forests, to obtain the boa constrictors, jaguars, parrots, toucans, and monkeys so accurately portrayed on Moche ceramics and jewelry.

Moche man, as he pictured himself in ceramic, was short and thickset. His head was long and narrow, with high cheekbones, wide mouth, hooked nose, and almond-shaped eyes. He cut his hair in bangs over his forehead, wore it long in the back, pierced his nose and ears, painted his face, and tattooed his arms and legs. His counterpart, Moche woman, was equally thickset. Her hair was worn long, and was often braided with colorful woolen strands. During ceremonial occasions her dress consisted of a multicolored woven smock heavily laden with long strands of beads. As colorful as her outfits were, however, men's ceremonial costumes were far richer, often highlighted by great plumes of feathers and topped by elaborate headdresses.

Primarily an agricultural society, the Moche extended their oases in the river valleys by building aqueducts to tap mountain rivers to feed hundreds of small irrigation ditches that led to their fields and orchards. Examples of these aqueducts, some still in use today, twist and turn for as long as seventy miles and must have required legions of laborers to haul the millions of cubic feet of earth needed to construct them. Into their fields the Moche poured earth and imported fertilizer to grow corn, peanuts, potatoes, melons, and a variety of other fruits and vegetables. Domesticated llama and alpaca were sources of meat and wool, and the cold Humboldt current, just offshore, provided the Moche with one of the richest fishing grounds on earth.

Besides canals and aqueducts, the Moche built massive temples, palaces, and pyramids out of rectangular sun-dried bricks, a material well suited to the arid climate of the north coast. Their most famous pyramid, known today as the Huaca del Sol, or Temple of the Sun, located in the Moche Valley, was constructed with an estimated 130 million bricks, using more than 4 million tons of clay, and covering twelve and a half acres of land. Ten thousand people may have lived at a single Moche pyramid complex at Pampa Grande, in Lambayeque, and at an estimated 750 manned lookout stations and stone ramparts at a Moche fortress near the town of Chepen, overlooking the Pacific. But despite the presence of these monuments and hundreds like them across the Andean cordillera, no one now knew their purpose, or much about the complex social organization that must have existed for these structures to have been built.

For all their apparent sophistication, the Moche were not known to have developed a writing system, not even glyphs such as served the Maya. The closest the Moche may have come to developing such a system were inscriptions painted on lima beans, believed by Rafael Larco Hoyle to have been a type of code or primitive script that permitted couriers to carry messages among tribal leaders. Fortunately for researchers, however, the Moche immortalized scenes of ritual and mythology on pots, bottles, and vases that they buried along with their dead. Indeed, almost all that was known about the Moche prior to the discoveries at Huaca Rajada was gleaned from these ceramics.

Except for artifacts that were strictly utilitarian, the most distinctive examples of Moche ceramics were easy to recognize because of their molded wishbone-shaped handles, known as "stirrup-spouts." Ranging in size from a tangerine to larger than a football, these ceramics depicted men, women, plants, animals, and anthropomorphic creatures engaged in an astonishing variety of activities that included fishing, hunting, combat, sexual acts, and elaborate ceremonies involving punishment, sacrifice, and celebration. Moche "portrait head vases," one form of stirrup-spout ceramics, were realistic enough in appearance for the subjects portrayed on them to have identifying wrinkles, warts, and moles. These finely wrought sculpted portraits were so imaginative that modern art collectors often mistook them for contemporary creations rather than two-thousand-year-old artifacts.

Little else was known about the Moche culture. Their civilization continued to build temples and pyramids for seven or eight centuries; then, for reasons not yet understood, the Moche vanished. Many archaeologists speculate that the end was brought about by an invasion of the Huari people from the southern mountain regions. Another school of archaeologists speculate that some natural disaster in the form of an earthquake or torrential rains known as El Ninos may have swept through the Moche kingdom and brought on massive flooding and starvation. However the end may have occurred, the Chimu replaced the Moche on the north coast, only to be conquered by the armies of the Inca Empire shortly after 1470.

As a young archaeologist and avid student of the Moche culture, Walter Alva reserved judgment on the question of what may have caused the sudden decline of the Moche civilization. Instead, he concentrated on an examination of the Moche culture through its ceramic legacy, the path his mentor, Max Diaz, a historian at the prestigious University of Trujillo, had recommended.

Alva considered Max Diaz his uncle, although they weren't, in fact, related. They first met when Alva was seven years old and his family moved from Cajamarca, a city high in the Andes mountains, to Trujillo, in the Moche Valley. Not long after his family arrived there, Walter's father, an engineer, and his mother, a schoolteacher, took their son to visit Diaz, who lived in the small town of Moche, just outside Trujillo. Despite the thirty-two-year difference in their ages, Alva and Diaz became inseparable. According to Alva's older brother, a physician currently practicing in Lima, the friendship endured because Diaz had three beautiful unmarried daughters. Alva, however, said it was because he loved to study history and Diaz had that rare gift to bring the subject alive, first in a child's imagination and later in a classroom.

During the hours Alva spent in Diaz's book-lined study or on field trips to the Moche pyramids, Diaz directed his young protégé away from the "book end" approach to studying the Moche. Instead, Diaz taught Alva to liken all Peruvian history to one long and unbroken continuum, and not to view the Moche as a separate civilization from the Inca or any other north-coast civilization. The earlier Chavin civilization ate, drank, and buried their dead much as the Moche did, and the Chimu crafted ceramics with stirrup-spout handles and used the temples and pyramids that the Moche had built. In Diaz's mind, the difference between the cultures lay in their distinctive approach to art. "Art to the Moche," Diaz said, echoing Larco Hoyle, "was their language. To understand Moche art is to understand their culture."

Diaz employed unusual teaching techniques by having Alva examine ceramic collections in a darkened room. In this way, Alva learned to distinguish Moche artistic style from that of other cultures merely by running his fingers over the surface of the pieces. Diaz also taught Alva how to catalog symbols and patterns that appeared on Moche ceramics, urging him to try to interpret and read these symbols in the context of the Moche culture and environment. By age twelve, Alva had become so adept at recognizing Moche artistic style that he could detect museum-quality forgeries. At age fifteen, Alva had surpassed even Diaz in his ability to identify recurring regional stylistic patterns, a talent, in the eyes of fellow high school students, akin to magic.

But Alva's training was not limited to his mentor's private collection of ceramics or to the even larger collection at the University of Trujillo. Diaz introduced Alva to the families of huaqueros operating in many of the north-coast river valleys. Though both Diaz and Alva were vigorously opposed to tomb looting, they kept on friendly terms with the huaqueros because they were the best source of information on Moche burial patterns and newly discovered Moche artifacts.

An important side trip on which Diaz took Alva was to the seaside village of Eten, where a few residents still knew words in Muchic, the ancient language of the north coast, and nearby ruins gave mute testament to the sheer power and size of the Moche kingdom in that area. It was here, in the Department of Lambayeque, an area virtually overlooked by early European treasure hunters, that Diaz believed a royal Moche burial would someday be found.

With Diaz's help, Alva became the youngest student to enter the archaeology department at the University of Trujillo. Introductions proved unnecessary, for most professors remembered Alva as the young boy who had been barred from entering the university museum because security guards had repeatedly caught Alva physically handling the ceramics on display. Now, at age seventeen, Alva was put in charge of the same museum collection and quickly became a rising star in the archaeological community.

Echoing many of Diaz's sentiments as well as those of

older and more established Moche scholars, young Alva presumed the Moche social structure and religious belief system to be similar to later, better known north-coast cultures. Farmers, warriors, priests, couriers, musicians, and artists by profession, the Moche were members of earth-cells, clans to which they belonged by blood ties. They carried the totem symbol of their clan on their shield, lance, or helmet when they went into battle or presented themselves before tribal and spiritual leaders in sacred ceremonies held high atop their enormous monuments.

Thus, in young Alva's emerging thesis, the spiritual and social lives of the Moche centered around their pyramids and the ceremonies conducted there. As with the Maya, the Aztecs, and countless other early civilizations, human sacrifice and cannibalism became a fundamental part of many of their ceremonies, a sacred obligation performed by priests for the welfare of all. Blood of the living, the Moche believed, nourished the spirits that governed the cosmos, just as the earth's riches fed, clothed, and protected mankind. By celebrating death, the Moche believed that they made life possible.

In this regard, the Moche excelled, exhibiting a special talent for turning ritual violence and sacrifice into high art. Iconographic evidence indicates that all the human and animal creatures the Moche portrayed in ceramic played symbolic roles in their sacred ceremonies. Ritual sacrifice, decapitation, and cannibalism appeared on Moche ceramic artwork like notes on a page of sheet music, leading Alva to believe that all art produced by the Moche had been created solely for religious or ceremonial use.

Among the bizarre cast of half-human and half-animal characters portrayed in Moche art was the almighty lord or king, who presided over their rich ceremonial and spiritual life. Nearly every north-coast archaeologist and student of Andean culture had ideas about what may or may not have constituted a Moche lord. The one Alva found the most intriguing was originated in 1974 by Dr. Christopher Donnan, based on his exhaustive study of the 125,000 photographs of Moche art and iconography he had assembled at UCLA for his landmark text, *Moche Art of Peru*.

Easy to recognize because of the bolts of lightning or rays that emanate from their heads and torsos, Donnan's Moche lords were always portrayed standing atop a throne perched on a massive pyramid, or sitting on a litter being carried in a procession. Most archaeologists claimed this lord to be no more than a product of some ancient artist's imagination: a mythical ruler whom the Moche used to explain their origins or to act as their spiritual bridge between life and death. Alva believed him to be a real man, a lord incarnate, the supreme ruler of an exotic cast of high priests and other members of the royal court.

Tantalizing as this theory was, no Moche scholar could prove it. Nor could scholars prove that the culture of the Moche was as large and technically sophisticated as Alva believed it must have been. None of the so-called Moche rulers' tombs had ever been found; nor had an archaeologist unearthed a single tool or relic that could be directly linked to one of their religious ceremonies. All the evidence archaeologists had to prove their theories were ceramic vases and isolated gold and silver ornaments held in private collections or on museum shelves, long ago stolen or looted from monuments or tombs. Moreover, as dealers charged higher and higher prices for quality Moche art, a new class of international antiquities buyers had replaced archaeologists and local collectors in the competition for the most recent discoveries.

Ironically, just as Alva graduated at the top of his class at the University of Trujillo, his mentor, Max Diaz, died; and with his death, Alva lost his enthusiasm for a career that measured success or failure on scholarly interpretations of ancient Moche iconography. Instead, Alva chose to specialize in earlier, less controversial north-coast cultures, where he believed he could make more significant contributions. He published two books in that area, took a job as assistant director at the Bruning Museum, and fathered two children. But in spite of the focus of his research and the pressure placed upon him as chief archaeological supervisor for a region as large as some countries, Alva honored the spirit of Max Diaz and the Moche culture in his heart, in the occasional letters or photographs he sent to Christopher Donnan at UCLA, and in the frequent lectures he delivered to schoolchildren at the Bruning.

Huaqueros had now located the tomb of a Moche lord—a tomb that could provide Alva and the Bruning Museum a chance to make an unparalleled contribution to Moche scholarship. But first Alva would have to recover the rest of the looted artifacts from huaqueros and locate the tomb while there was still something to excavate.

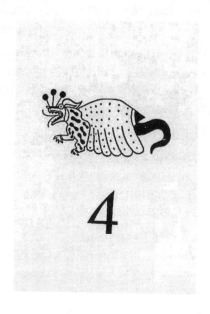

4

Exhausted yet unable to sleep, Alva telephoned the Bruning Museum and left a message for his assistant archaeologist, twenty-six-year-old Luis Chero Zurita, or Lucho, to pack provisions and equipment and meet him at police headquarters in Chiclayo early the next morning. Once Lucho arrived, Alva briefed him about the events of the night. They then accompanied PIP investigators on a sunrise raid of the Bernal family home, a six-room stucco-and-cinder-block farmhouse less than a mile from their ultimate destination, the pyramids of Huaca Rajada.

Minutes after the caravan of eight policemen, the two archaeologists, and the Bruning driver, Benedicto, reached the Bernal farmhouse, Alva made an appalling discovery. Lingering beside the museum van as the police prepared to raid the Bernal house, Alva noticed an unusual shape protruding from the mud at the bottom of an irrigation ditch that ran the length of the sugarcane fields bordering the house. By inclination and training Alva recognized the unusual shape as a potsherd. Leaning down to take a closer look, he quickly noticed that this wasn't the only potsherd in the mud, or the only unusual shape in the canal. Heaps of red-clay potsherds and corroded chunks of green copper and brown metal littered the canal bottom and banks of the irrigation ditch.

Unless Alva was mistaken, Ernil and his men had cleaned their loot in the canal, separating the marketable items before smashing the rest and leaving them scattered across the bottom of the ditch. Marketable items, in the eyes of Ernil and his men, consisted of anything made of silver, gold, or engraved stone. Refuse consisted of the shattered remains of Moche pots and vases, ornaments, textiles, and bone, the kind of material valuable to no one except an archaeologist.

Assistant Police Chief Temoche told Alva to ignore the smashed ceramics and concentrate on helping him and his men search the house and adjacent buildings. But the archaeologist in Alva could not abandon the potsherds, and he and Lucho proceeded to climb down the canal embankment to collect as many as they could find. Any uncertainty about the origin of the potsherds vanished when one of Temoche's men accidently stepped on the shattered remains of a Moche stirrup-spout pot in a second refuse heap at the rear of the house, between a latrine and the sugarcane fields. By Alva's conservative estimate, huaqueros had smashed more than 250 ceramic vases and an equal number of copper ornaments and jewelry: the tribute, Alva supposed, that regional Moche leaders may have paid to their lord at the time of his burial.

Investigators later confirmed what Alva had suspected the moment he came upon the potsherds. He and the police had arrived too late to claim the remaining Moche artifacts. Evidence from inside the house as well as eyewitness testimony from the huaquero who had turned on his associates indicated that police had recovered only a small fraction of the plundered treasures that were removed from the tomb; the remaining artifacts would soon be making their way to antiquities dealers in Trujillo and Lima, if they hadn't been moved there already. Ernil's father, Carlos Bernal, the only occupant of the house besides Ernil's mother and one of his young children, refused to provide details that might lead to the hiding place of Ernil and his eight brothers, or the remaining rice sacks full of antiquities.

By the time investigators completed their search of the house and turned their attention to the location of the tomb itself, the sun had risen and the pyramids of Huaca Rajada could be seen clearly silhouetted on the horizon. The two largest of the three pyramids rose above the fields as European cathedrals must have once towered over medieval cities, their mute tobacco-brown bricks casting a pale hue over the emerald green of the sugarcane fields surrounding them. The third pyramid, by far the smallest, was weatherworn to the shape of a mound, barely visible behind a grove of eucalyptus trees at its base.

As Alva and the police drove along the main road toward Huaca Rajada, the vast mass of the pyramid complex became immediately apparent: a rectangle the size of a football field, raised to the height of a twenty-story building; a second peak about the same height, also fiat-topped, and separated from its neighbor by a narrow road that cut like an arrow between the adjoining sugarcane fields; and the brown mound of the smallest pyramid. This third pyramid was so small by comparison to the other two that visitors to Huaca Rajada seldom recognized the mound as a pyramid at all, mistaking it for an entrance ramp or portal leading to the neighboring pyramids.

Neither Alva nor Temoche was prepared for the sight that greeted them at the base of the pyramids. Huaqueros covered the top and sides of the smallest of the three; others clung to the sides or stood high atop the neighboring two, completely indifferent to the arrival of the police. Teams of looters nearer the road heaved pickaxes and shovels, or even used their bare hands, to poke and pry among the pyramid bricks for any gold trinkets or beads that Ernil and his men might have overlooked. Everyone from the nearby village of Sipan, perhaps even from as far away as the Pomalca farm cooperative on the road to Chiclayo, must have heard the news of the Moche treasure and come to seek his fortune between Huaca Rajada's ancient bricks.

Temoche raced into the pyramid complex with his siren howling, the wheels of the patrol car sending up a swirl of dust on the narrow unpaved road as they screeched to a halt. When it was clear that the staccato blare of the siren was having no affect on the huaqueros, Temoche ordered his men to shoot bursts of automatic fire into the air. Huaqueros at the top of all three pyramids fired a volley of shots back, temporarily forcing Temoche and his men to take cover. Benedicto immediately put the Volkswagen van into reverse, pulling back into the safety of a nearby grove of trees.

Usually the mere presence of an outsider was enough to scatter huaqueros. But here at Huaca Rajada, Temoche had to send his men into their tunnels before the looters gave up their positions. Even then, so many looters had converged on Huaca Rajada that Temoche couldn't begin to round up all of them or keep them from scrambling down the sides of the pyramid and escaping into the sugarcane fields. Using a loudspeaker attached to the patrol car, Temoche ordered the remaining villagers back to their homes.

A half hour later, amid protests from villagers unwilling to abandon the site and the cries of a lost child seeking her parents, Temoche ordered one team of patrolmen to clear a space beside the eucalyptus trees for a base camp, while a second team began the dangerous and time-consuming task of flushing out any huaqueros who had lingered inside the tunnels. Much to the credit of the police, neither villagers nor patrolmen were injured; and except for a cave-in that left one looter temporarily trapped inside his own tunnel and the blood-stained corpse of one of Ernil's partners in another, the huaqueros had also escaped serious injury.

Ignoring Temoche's orders to remain beside the museum van, Alva wasted no time reaching the central platform of the shortest of the three pyramids, a rectangle about the size of a city block. Heaps of backfill, scattered piles of clay brick, and countless gouges, scars, and holes in the platform convinced Alva that this indeed had been the focus of the major looting activity. And if the size of the crowd gathering just outside the police perimeter was any indication, huaqueros would have razed the entire top off the pyramid had Alva and the police arrived any later.

Undaunted, Alva and Lucho set about looking for the one tunnel among many where Ernil and his men had uncovered the burial chamber, not an easy task considering that every few feet a hole had been carved into the pyramid platform. Help arrived at twelve-thirty P.M., in the unlikely guise of Mrs. Mercedes Zapata, the chief police informant in their case against Ernil and his men and Huaca Rajada's self-proclaimed "landlord."

In truth, Mrs. Zapata, a mother and grandmother, had no legal claims to Huaca Rajada besides those of a squatter. Unable to rent rooms in the nearby village, she and her husband had chosen the nearest and most convenient piece of unused land, "borrowing" clay bricks from the top of one of the pyramids to build a chicken coop, rabbit hutch, and three-room house. Police ignored her presence at the site because so few visitors ever bothered to come to Huaca Rajada and because Mrs. Zapata hadn't built her house on top of one of the pyramids but beside one.

Mrs. Zapata's house didn't turn out to be nearly as significant as her rabbit hutch. She had used the natural contours of the bricks at the base of the shortest pyramid to provide the hutch's bottom and backing, thus saving on expensive building materials and providing her three brown rabbits the opportunity to burrow into the cool and shaded interior of the pyramid. Alva and the police could well imagine her surprise when, the previous March, Mrs. Zapata looked into her rabbit hutch and saw a shiny gold bead. Each morning another gold bead appeared: compelling evidence that she had raised rabbits that passed "golden pellets."

Ricardo, Mrs. Zapata's eldest son, enlightened his superstitious mother about her misconceptions, which was how her family later got into trouble with Ernil Bernal. Between growing seasons at the farm cooperative, Ricardo and his friends began to tunnel into Huaca Rajada to look for the source of the beads. From April through November 1986, they carved two tunnels into the eastern side of the central platform and reopened a tunnel that huaqueros had abandoned years earlier. Among the many curious discoveries they made was a basketful of copper ornaments that appeared to have been covering bones from an ancient burial. Ernil Bernal learned about what had been found when Ricardo tried unsuccessfully to sell his copper ornaments to a jewelry store in Chiclayo. Ernil and his men had then used their muscle to try to push Mrs. Zapata and her son off the site, threatening to kill one or the other if they turned to the police.

Alva believed Mrs. Zapata for two reasons. Upon later police questioning, she took Alva and the police into her house at the foot of the pyramid and showed them examples of the copper ornaments she had described. Mrs. Zapata also took Alva and Lucho directly to the tunnel where Ernil and his men had penetrated the burial chamber.

Using tunneling methods passed on from one generation to the next, Ernil and his men had cut a shaft straight down into the pyramid. They then began to probe a larger and larger area under the pyramid platform by carving horizontal passages off the main shaft, much like the roots of a tree. Discovery of the burial chamber took place in the third horizontal passage they had carved; it pointed east and extended about sixteen feet from the vertical shaft. Ernil's men then enlarged their main tunnel to accommodate more than one huaquero before cutting steps into the side of the vertical shaft to provide an easier means of access and to accelerate the removal of great quantities of clay brick and other refuse.

Within hours of discovering the burial chamber, Ernil's men had cut a second vertical shaft connecting the burial chamber to a fourth horizontal passage, just large enough for Chalo, Ernil's friend, to squeeze his shoulders through. By this time, however, much of the area around the burial chamber looked like the earth under an anthill, and huaqueros had begun to use ropes, buckets, and a bamboo ladder to provide greater access in and out of the pyramid and to speed up the removal of brick.

Availing himself of this same bamboo ladder, Alva would go alone into the tunnel, careful not to lose his balance and fall the twenty-three feet straight down. At the bottom, in a boot-shaped chamber about the size of the Bruning's Volkswagen van, Alva hesitated. Years of experience in huaqueros' tunnels had taught him that tombs have a sour, almost acrid odor all their own, even ones that are thousands of years old. Ernil's tunnel had that special odor.

Alva lit the lantern he was carrying, lifted it over his head, and followed the tunnel straight back until he reached the spot where Ernil and his men must have penetrated the burial chamber. A preliminary examination revealed a room about seven feet square and nine feet high.

Hours earlier that day, at the Bernal farmhouse, Alva had been able to examine heaps of ceramic potsherds. But in this brick-lined cavity that had once been a tomb, nothing remained except bones and pottery crushed into powder and the multiple scars from the heavy, blunt tools Ernil and his men had used to probe the burial chamber's limits.

To police investigators, Alva emerged from the huaqueros' tunnel as clear-headed and composed as the archaeologist they had seen vanish inside. But colleagues close to Alva knew his profound sense of anger and loss. He had arrived too late to retrieve the bulk of the plundered artifacts from the Bernal house or to save any information that could have been obtained from a proper excavation of the tomb. His only option now was to salvage what he could from the plundered chamber, increase the police patrols of the site, then hire temporary laborers to haul crushed brick and sand to the top of the platform and fill the huaqueros' tunnels.

His "key to the Moche culture," as the press later called the plundered burial chamber at Huaca Rajada, had been torn from his hands.

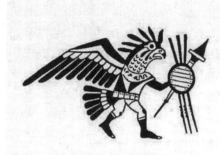

5

As Alva and the police were inspecting the vacant burial chamber at Huaca Rajada, Italian-born antiquities collector Enrico Poli was crossing the border into the Moche Valley on a clandestine mission to purchase the most important collection of looted pre-Columbian art to reach the black market in more than a century.

A tall, imperious man, whose profile and arrogance reminded associates of a Roman emperor, the fifty-nine-year-old Poli had held a special place in the antiquities underground since his arrival in Lima in 1954, and his subsequent rise to prominence as a financier and hotel operator. Poli's friends claim that he came to Peru from Sicily as a cook for an international mining corporation and used his meager earnings to invest in real estate and precious metals. His rivals, however, paint a different picture: that he had fled Italy to avoid an impending jail sentence and used alleged Mafia connections to set himself up in the Lima hotel business. Poli himself says that he had arrived in Lima penniless, and that he had let nothing stop him in an all-consuming effort to corner the Peruvian market in colonial gold and silver antiquities. He also describes how often he convinced parish priests at small missions in the Andes mountains to trade a sixteenth-century silver altar or collection of colonial gold reliquaries for a Frigidaire refrigerator, activities that resulted in jail time for Poli in three different prisons. Eventually Poli's tastes shifted from colonial gold and silver to pre-Columbian ornaments and rare ceramics. Villagers from remote settlements in the mountains or small villages on the north coast began to send messengers to his private, heavily fortified compound in Lima to tell him of important tombs or sites that had been looted. With their help and his discerning eye, he soon amassed a collection of antiquities that rivaled and then surpassed those of the national museums. Poli never claimed to have the largest collection of pre-Columbian and colonial treasures in all of Peru. He had the best.

Now, as Alva was trying to secure Huaca Rajada from further looting, Poli was motoring across the 360-mile expanse of sand and river valleys that ran between Lima and Trujillo. Under normal circumstances, "Don Poli," as huaqueros and "providers" knew him, would never consider making a personal appearance at the home of someone besides a major distributor. He would have asked that the individual pieces be brought to him in Lima for his personal inspection or that he be provided with Polaroid photographs of the pieces to examine. But Poli trusted his instincts in this case, gambling on there being some truth to the rumor that a royal Moche burial had been unearthed somewhere on the north coast. Hours earlier, he had seen and purchased the first items that huaqueros claimed had come out of this tomb. And in all the years Poli had monitored the market, he had never heard stories of such fabulous artifacts: matching gold and silver ceremonial tools and moon-shaped masks depicting creatures half-human and half-animal. Poli instantly recognized the pieces as Moche, just as he recognized the name of the archaeologist who was helping police launch an investigation into the origins of the artifacts. In the field of pre-Columbian art, serious scholars, collectors, and traders all knew one another. Poli had visited the Bruning Museum to see its Moche and Chavin ceramics and Alva had traveled to Lima to photograph and study Poli's equally magnificent collections.

To hear Poli tell the story, news of the looting at Huaca Rajada had reached him even before police closed in on the rice sack of Moche treasure at the Bernal farmhouse—a sack, Poli contends, that had been ear-marked for sale in Lima before the police turned it over to Alva. In order to make up for the loss, "providers" in Trujillo agreed to send sample pieces from the contents of a rice sack assigned to them. Poli purchased these samples for eight hundred dollars from his Lima contact the moment he laid eyes on them: six solid-gold triangles, about eight inches long and three inches wide, said to be links from a massive necklace that formed a giant circle of gold around the neck of a Moche lord. Each link contained approximately a quarter of an ounce of the precious metal, polished to a luster that caught the light. Using a high degree of care and skill, Moche craftsmen had cut the links from a solid sheet of hammered gold, crimped the ends to form a perfect geometric pattern, then polished the pieces over and over again until they were satin-smooth.

Poli realized the significance of the richness of the initial offering. But that didn't mean the entire collection would be his. Quite the opposite. Huaqueros never sent providers their important pieces until all their minor pieces had been sold. And in order to be considered a potential customer for the better items, Poli had to purchase all the pieces offered him, including fakes, reproductions, and anything else that might be included as part of the first transactions. Dealers traditionally used their one or two best pieces to clear their inventory of second and third-quality art. Nor could his contacts be trusted to make him their sole client, or even one of ten.

Because Poli hadn't the patience or resources to let two or more dealers package such an important collection, he broke the rules, pressuring his Lima contacts until they revealed the names of their counterparts in Trujillo.

Excited at the prospect of having the collection all to himself, Poli did not return home before heading off to Trujillo. Instead, he stopped at the bank to collect the cash he estimated he might need to purchase the important pieces. His bank, however, couldn't cash his forty-thousand-dollar check in anything but small-denomination bills, and he had to purchase three suitcases to haul forty bundles of cash to Trujillo. Poli had every reason to fear taking such a large amount over the Pan- American highway at night. He came upon his first thief trying to steal his parked car when he returned from the bank carrying his suitcases. Luckily for Poli, the thief ran off, never realizing that Poli had a small fortune in Moche gold in the trunk of his green Peugeot, and suitcases containing bundles of cash under his arms.

More than seven hours later, pistol in hand, suitcases in the backseat, Poli crisscrossed Trujillo's cobblestone streets until he came to an unassuming colonial building on a quiet boulevard north of the Plaza de Armas. He entered the building through an arched stone passage which led to an open-air courtyard and knocked on an unmarked service door. A child answered and took Poli into the kitchen to see his father. Pereda, the name by which Poli and his contacts referred to this important north-coast provider, was a short, stocky former policeman, clearly more at ease speaking to huaqueros at a small cantina in a remote village than to an art collector of Poli's status. Poli knew him by reputation, as Pereda knew Poli by reputation.

Pereda seldom handled first-rate materials. Three years earlier, Poli had considered purchasing a piece from him, but changed his mind when Pereda demanded that Poli buy the piece in combination with two others, clearly forgeries. But Poli held no grudge. Antiquities traders handling pieces on consignment employed all kinds of practices to make an important sale, including mixing beads from one necklace with beads from another in order to make it seem more exotic. Poli believed he knew all the tricks of the trade.

Besides, one of Pereda's associates had helped Poli to obtain the contents of a Moche tomb in Balsar, a rich archaeological site in the Jequetepeque Valley, south of Lambayeque. These artifacts were the most important gold ornaments in Poli's collection, perhaps the most significant Moche antiquities in private hands. Poli obviously couldn't afford to offend anyone in the trade.

As custom demanded, Poli and Pereda spoke casually about everything from politics to the recent cold spell, and even shared a glass of vintage Pisco, a hundred-proof liquor made on Peru's south coast, before Pereda spoke about the Huaca Rajada treasures. Like those in Lima, the pieces he had on consignment were meant to test the market rather than to generate a substantial amount of immediate income. The sums the artifacts raised would be used to help him and his clients until the police investigation had ended and they could put more artifacts on the market. Above all, extreme caution was to be exercised at all times.

Pereda then sent his son into the next room to retrieve the artifacts. They were presented to Poli in two brown paper sacks that resembled shopping bags. The first sack contained four golden peanut beads and a pair of silver and gold nose rings. The second sack contained a massive moon-shaped back flap made of solid gold, presumably hung on the belt of a Moche lord to cover his buttocks, much like armor on a medieval knight.

Poli told Pereda that the pieces were mediocre, though both he and Pereda knew them to be magnificent. Using the same high degree of care and detail apparent on the necklace links Poli had purchased back in Lima, Moche craftsmen had hammered the peanut beads, nose rings, and back flap from a sheet of nearly pure gold. To the eye, the pieces appeared quite substantial, but to the touch, paper thin.

Pereda put a price of twenty-five hundred dollars on the pieces. Poli accepted, but a problem soon developed. Poli expected to see more pieces, and Pereda appeared reluctant to acknowledge that he had more to sell, or knew how to get them.

Poli expressed disappointment, for he already had two similar artifacts in his collection of looted treasures from Balsar. The national museums also had six or seven comparable pieces, and the Metropolitan Museum of Art in New York had an exact duplicate. As a connoisseur of Moche art, Poli expected something so unique that it could only have been discovered in the tomb of a Moche lord.

Pereda confessed that more spectacular pieces had been unearthed, though he hadn't seen them personally. His clients had chosen to restrict their sales until the police investigation had ended. He had only one more artifact available, and this couldn't be shown unless he first obtained his clients' permission.

Either Pereda had employed a clever sales strategy to raise interest in the artifact, or he had another buyer in mind. Poli couldn't be certain, so he told Pereda to contact his clients if he wished to continue to conduct business with him.

Less than an hour later, three men appeared in the red-tiled courtyard to speak to Pereda. Pereda excused himself, and the four had a heated conversation in view of Poli and Pereda's son. Poli again wondered if this was a clever sales strategy.

Finally, the eldest of Pereda's three visitors, a man whom the PIP believed to have been David Aladena Bernal, Ernil's brother, left the courtyard and returned a few moments later, about the length of time required to go to the street and remove a package from the trunk of a car. He was carrying a brown paper parcel under his arm. Pereda took the parcel and rejoined Poli in the kitchen. Poli removed a string from around the package and opened it on the table.

On his trip to Trujillo, Poli had imagined Pereda presenting him modeled gold or silver figurines, vestments, and ceremonial artifacts as rich in splendor as those Pizarro and his men had plundered from the Inca Empire. Here was such a piece, made all the more special because Moche craftsmen had created it twelve hundred years before Pizarro and his men had ever come to Peru: a palm-sized golden statue of a Moche lord, its eyes encrusted with lapis lazuli, its golden crown sparkling in the afternoon sunlight. In one of its hands the miniature lord held a finely carved shield, whose emblem represented some ancient clan affiliation; in its other, a gold pyramid-shaped rattle, similar to one depicted in Moche art and iconography held in the hand of the presiding lord in a Moche sacrificial ceremony.

Poli declined Pereda's initial price of $150,000 and

proposed $30,000. Pereda countered, and Poli came back with $50,000 and then $65,000, the highest he had ever agreed to pay for a single pre-Columbian treasure that had come to the black market in Trujillo. Pereda pushed Poli up to $75,000.

Both Pereda and Poli knew that a record had been broken, but neither could be sure if the record was for the price offered to a north-coast antiquities trader for a single Moche burial figurine, or the price offered for anything made by the Moche. Pieces as exquisite as the miniature lord had never been put on the black market.

Before the sale could be consummated, however, Poli first had to hand over seventy-five thousand dollars in cash, far more than he had left in his three suitcases. Pereda told him he had to have the full amount right now or his clients would leave. Further negotiations resulted in Poli squeezing an hour from Pereda and his clients: the time he needed to get to a branch of his bank or stop at the home of an associate, a rich hotel owner on the outskirts of Trujillo.

Furious that a man of his stature should be pressured in this manner, Poli made a point not to rush to the bank and back. Nor was he concerned when the bank hadn't the cash reserves he needed and he had to wait until arrangements could be made to transfer the funds from a second, larger bank. By the time he returned to Pereda's house, an hour and fifteen minutes after he had left, Poli had an entire car packed with small bills in cardboard boxes, suitcases, and shopping bags. But thoughts of the precious miniature gold lord, soon to be his, overcame Poli's sense of humiliation.

Pereda opened the gate into the courtyard only after Poli had repeatedly knocked. Even then, he refused Poli entrance into the house but made him stand in the courtyard. His clients had agreed to wait one hour. Poli's tardiness had cost him the miniature Moche lord.

Incensed, Poli made threats he later regretted.

The figurine he had agreed to purchase represented only one item out of a collection estimated to contain 475 pieces. His outburst cost him the privilege of conducting business with Pereda and, at the same time, created an opening for his archrival to step in. Poli knew this to be the case because he noticed his rival's aluminum crutches propped up against the refrigerator in the kitchen when Pereda excused himself and returned inside. Fred Drew, an expatriate American and a trader in illegal exports in Lima, had fractured his knees by falling into a huaqueros' shaft at a Moche site outside Trujillo. His presence at Pereda's meant but one thing: Unless Drew could be stopped, the contents of the Moche tomb would be shipped overseas and sold through the international antiquities underground.

PART 2

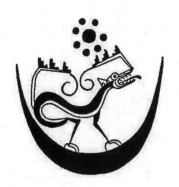

HOUSE OF
THE MOON

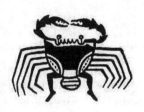

6

For reasons the archaeologist chose to keep to himself, Alva postponed his March 2, 1987, plans to call in temporary laborers to fill the huaqueros' tunnels and seal the looted pyramid platform at Huaca Rajada. Instead, on March 10, Alva elected to pitch a tent on a pedestal of clay bricks above the entrance to Ernil's abandoned tunnel, requested that investigators post two full-time patrolmen to police the site, and, from sunrise to sunset, held a month-long self-imposed exile in the looted burial chambers.

Lucho protested the postponement for the same reasons that police requested that Alva seal the pyramid platform and return to the museum. Each hour Alva and the patrolmen remained at Huaca Rajada increased the likelihood of an armed incursion from huaqueros. Far better to use police personnel and Alva's expertise to protect another structure, Lucho maintained, than to squander their resources on a pyramid that had already been plundered. Moreover, the INC in Lima had recently promoted Lucho to the rank of supervising archaeologist and had authorized his transfer to a city in the highlands east of Trujillo. Lucho delayed having Alva sign his transfer papers until his superior could recuperate from bronchitis and hire another assistant. Now that Alva had recovered, Lucho expected Alva to be interviewing replacements, not living in a vacant huaqueros' tunnel at Huaca Rajada.

Like the police, Lucho assumed that Alva's motives at the site were not constructive. In their eyes, Alva, at the expense of police and museum resources, had chosen to remain at Huaca Rajada to lament the loss of the tomb and ponder its impact upon his campaign to protect the monuments under his supervision. But they couldn't begrudge his contemplation of the hopeless nature of the mission he had undertaken.

In truth, however, Alva had little or no interest in spending time in self-pity. Though he lamented the loss of the contribution he might have been able to make to Moche scholarship, he had chosen to remain at the site to marshal as much information as he could from the looted burial chamber and, later, to investigate a number of curious archaeological anomalies about the pyramid's construction. Huaqueros had provided him a rare opportunity to scrutinize a cross-section of the pyramid and Alva couldn't bring himself to fill the shafts and seal the platform until he had a chance to explain to himself how a royal Moche burial had been unearthed at a site considered to be non-Moche.

Alva's initial questions concerned the origins and purpose of the pyramid complex itself. Like other archaeologists and treasure hunters who had examined Huaca Rajada on routine expeditions to Lambayeque, Alva had overlooked it as the site for an important burial because an examination of the building materials, potsherds, and other surface collections indicated that the three pyramids had been built around the year A.D. 1100 by the Chimu, a post-Moche civilization not known to have buried their leaders inside pyramids.

First appearances, as Max Diaz had taught Alva, could be deceptive because a pyramid complex as old as Huaca Rajada underwent considerable changes after its construction. Besides the number of large pits and tunnels that looters carved into the pyramids, all three faced an even more forceful enemy in the form of torrential rains from El Ninos. In 1983, for example, El Ninos had turned much of Lambayeque into a lake. Alva and a crew of schoolchildren and staff members had had to wade through the Bruning Museum to retrieve Inca mummies and pre-Hispanic ceramics stored in the basement, "a museum director," Alva once said, "literally bearing the weight of the past on his back."

Based on research conducted at the Moche Valley by Michael Moseley, an archaeologist from the University of Florida, Alva knew that Huaca Rajada must have withstood hundreds of El Nino storms that had trimmed at least twelve feet off the tops and sides of the pyramids. Without Moche caretakers to cut back the growth of trees and vines or to renew their original adobe skin, the steep sides of the pyramids became cracked, the ramps and platforms connecting them worn and overgrown, until the earthen pyramid complex resembled blocks of melted chocolate.

But in spite of the rains and the periodic attacks by huaqueros, the outlines of an enormous religious and ceremonial complex could be clearly seen. Just beneath a blanket of sugarcane fields, the road leading to it extended twelve miles to the east, in the direction of Pampa Grande, the site of a Moche city that many archaeologists believed to have once been the center of a state holding sway over the Lambayeque Valley. In typical pre-Inca tradition, a ramp, much like one seen in a contemporary sports stadium, marked the entrance to Huaca Rajada. From this ramp, laid out in careful north-south alignment, the pyramids ascended in a series of steps, or terraces, leading to the central platform containing a canopied throne and sanctuary. In such a reserved compound there would have moved servants, concubines, warriors, and priests, all attending the sovereign. Presumably, it was here where the Moche lord accepted homage and tribute and performed his specified ceremonial duties. Like an Egyptian pharaoh, he was considerably more than just a king; he was a god in his own lifetime, descended from heaven.

Actual construction of a pyramid may have taken more than one generation, and required each community to contribute hundreds of men to fashion the clay bricks and hundreds more to haul them to the site. Unaided by the wheel, laborers passed the fresh bricks hand-to-hand to workmen, who stacked them like bread loaves in wide and distinct vertical stacks that abutted but did not bind, each higher than the previous one. As the platform and attached ramps rose higher and higher, scaffolding appeared as a roost for plasterers. A final coat of mud and sand was applied to protect the pyramid's sloping sides and seal its level platforms. Here at Huaca Rajada, so much mud and clay were used that a lake had formed about three quarters of a mile to the south of the pyramids, the result of the enormous pit laborers had carved out of the earth to remove building materials.

Having never had an opportunity to authenticate a royal Moche burial in one of these pyramids, archaeologists had no clear idea of what to expect; but a reasonable conclusion based on available evidence from Loma Negra, Balsar, and other looted sites was that only at a ruler's passing was a chamber carved out of a raised platform, pyramid, or ceremonial site to accommodate his body. Using cutting tools, measuring devices, and other instruments, Moche craftsmen cut a hole into which they placed the lord along with the burial goods and sacrifices that accompanied him. Above this hole or chamber, they laid down a canopy of beams, covered it with straw matting, and then covered the matting with bricks and rubble and sealed the top.

Following Andean tradition, the Moche lord would not have gone alone into death but would have been accompanied by wives and servants who were to continue to serve the "living corpse" in the afterlife. In the same tradition, the living did not feel safe until they had placed a barrier, either mountains or desert, between themselves and the dead. A pyramid, in this sense, was the "mountain of the desert," as Alva called it, the natural place for a ruler of importance to be interred. Because of the high status of the deceased, priests may have retired the pyramid from use and moved their religious headquarters to a new location.

Based on excavations in the Viru Valley under the direction of the Institute of Andean Research, Alva could assume that as many as three or four concubines or servants and large amounts of offerings in ceramic pots may have been buried alongside the coffin of the Moche lord. In one such excavation, a young man had apparently been sacrificed and placed on top of a cane coffin containing a high-ranking Moche priest. Two young girls were buried at the head and foot of his coffin, and a young male child was discovered underneath. Inside the coffin were placed large wooden scepters, shell necklaces, and copper ornaments, though none as rich in precious metals as those the police had seized from the Bernals.

Alva's initial interests at Huaca Rajada, however, lay less in the burial chamber itself than in the type of bricks used in building the pyramid, one of the most accepted keys archaeologists employed to differentiate between a Moche and a Chimu structure. In this respect, the work of

Donald McClelland, a research associate of Dr. Christopher Donnan, became invaluable. His analysis of brick typology at Pacatnamu, a complex of fifty truncated pyramids overlooking the Pacific Ocean, revealed the majority of Moche bricks to be mold-made, approximately eleven inches long, seven and a half inches wide, and four and a half inches high. The later Chimu bricks appeared to be shaped either by hand or by a flat tool. These measured approximately thirteen inches long, seven and a half inches wide, and four and a half inches high. Periodic rains that liquefied the clay mixture, along with the intense heat from the sun, made both set of bricks as hard as concrete.

On Alva's previous visits to Huaca Rajada, he had noted that the bricks that composed the outer, or top, layer of all three pyramids were those of the Chimu civilization: rough-hewn irregular rectangles that were longer and narrower than their Moche counterparts. Yet the bricks Alva now examined in the burial chamber were clearly smaller and not rough-hewn, but perfectly shaped rectangles, formed by pouring adobe into individual molds, as the Moche did.

McClelland himself would later visit Huaca Rajada and validate Alva's observations, which were further confirmed by the realization, early in his examination of the looter's tunnels, that Moche craftsmen had left their indelible imprint on some of the bricks, much the way an architect puts a cornerstone on a building. In the bricks massed in long strips on the north side of the Huaca Rajada platform, they had scratched circles, half-moons, cat's eyes and a nose, all symbols used on their ceramics. In one brick, even the handprint of the Moche craftsman had been preserved. Alva, who couldn't resist the temptation to splay his own hand across this brick, had an eerie sensation when he discovered that his fingers perfectly matched those of the dead man.

Examinations of brick from the tunnels and pits that the Bernal brothers had cut into the platform revealed further examples of Chimu masonry, fire pits, and potsherds on the top layer, and Moche craftsmanship on the bottom layers, leading Alva to ultimately conclude that all three pyramids may have originally been Moche structures.

Alva knew he shouldn't have been surprised by this revelation, but he was. Research at other pre-Inca and Inca pyramid sites along the coast supported his findings and highlighted one of Max Diaz's long-held convictions that the more rulers rebuilt temples and pyramids on the same spots over the centuries, the more sacred those sites became. Alva and the others who had come to Huaca Rajada had been tricked by a shell game perpetrated some twelve hundred or more years earlier. This had been the reason that the Moche lord's tomb had previously gone undetected.

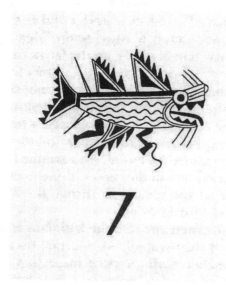

7

Despite El Nino rains and the depredations of the looters, Alva was able to sketch a contour map that clearly indicated that the smallest of the original structures had been a flat-topped multi-leveled pyramid, supported on a rectangular base about half the size of a football field and rising to the height of a three-story building. Later analysis of construction techniques and core samples taken from the huaqueros' tunnels revealed that the pyramid began as a small rectangular platform and was subsequently enlarged both horizontally and vertically through numerous renovations over a period of three hundred or more years.

Like the other two pyramids, it was orientated on a north-south axis, and in its present configuration had a long, low platform extending from its north side. Another low and somewhat shorter platform extending from its south side contained small rooms. A third, or "main," platform rising between the other two had presumably been the foundation for a small temple or throne room that once crowned the pyramid structure.

Keeping this in mind, Alva noticed a striking contrast between the placement inside the pyramid where he imagined the Moche would have buried their leader and the location where huaqueros had uncovered a royal tomb. Measurements confirmed the burial chamber to be on the far northwest corner of the main platform, approximately fifteen feet from the outside face of the pyramid. Regardless of the use later civilizations may have made of the pyramid or the various renovations that had taken place, the Moche had clearly buried a leader of exalted importance here. In view of his stature and the wealth of treasures that accompanied his burial, Alva assumed that the Moche would have buried him in the center of the main platform, not off to one side of the temple or throne room, a place more befitting a lesser lord or priest.

Having exhausted any clues he had obtained from a study of the outside of the pyramid, Alva turned his attention to the plundered chamber itself. A close inspection uncovered the telltale remains of wooden beams that must have once acted as a canopy or roof above the lord's resting place. Sockets for supporting posts had been cut into bricks laid sometime earlier, confirming Alva's expectation that the chamber had indeed been carved out of a preexisting platform on the pyramid. A nine-foot space between the chamber roof and the top of the pyramid provided more than adequate room for the ceramics that Alva had discovered smashed in the irrigation canal and for other animal or human sacrifices made at the time of the burial.

Yet an exploration of a tunnel immediately behind this chamber revealed another set of sockets, or a second smaller chamber seven feet beneath and two feet to the north of the first. Alva initially assumed that this chamber had once contained a sacrificial burial or a cache of ceramics similar to those found in the royal burial excavated in the Viru Valley. But in the Viru Valley, the burials and artifacts that accompanied the primary interment completely surrounded the coffin. At Huaca Rajada, many tons of brick separated the two chambers, suggesting that one of them may have been hundreds of years older than the other.

A few of the tunnels in the easternmost portion of the platform appeared to contain similar chambers: each at another level in the pyramid and each of about the same proportions as the first two. Each chamber also revealed evidence of smashed pottery and sockets for a roof. But here, as elsewhere, huaqueros had used such blunt instruments to cut shafts into the chambers, and then been in such a hurry to clean them out, that Alva hadn't a clue as to what the chambers may or may not have contained.

What was certain was that huaqueros had carved far more tunnels into the plundered platform than any one or two teams in the recent past could have created. The looters had sunk more than eight large shafts, twice that number of minor shafts or tunnels, and countless smaller holes or openings, leading Alva to suspect that huaqueros had been looting Huaca Rajada since before Ernil and his men had been born.

Alva also couldn't ignore the fact that neighboring pyramids on the road to Pampa Grande hadn't been touched. Unless huaqueros had known from legend or past experience that some important burial had been inside this pyramid, they wouldn't have taken the time or the trouble to concentrate on the site.

Mrs. Zapata shared the little information she had about the tunnels with Alva. According to her, most of the looting had taken place before her arrival at the site in the late 1950s. Villagers told stories about looting that had taken place in 1922 and 1923, and large amounts of gold and silver that had been unearthed. Huaqueros had apparently stopped their tunneling for fear of evil spirits believed to cast their spell on anyone trespassing in their huaca. Mrs. Zapata also told Alva that the name Huaca Rajada, meaning "Temple of the Cracks" in Spanish, was a relatively recent name for the site. Earlier residents had called it Sipan, or "House of the Moon," a designation she claimed came from *Si* meaning "moon" in the ancient north-coast language of Muchic, *p*, a possessive article, and *an*, meaning "house."

References to the monuments of Huaca Rajada as Sipan could be neither confirmed nor rejected because contemporary anthropologists and linguists knew next to nothing about the Muchic language. However, many Andean scholars in the early 1950s believed that the Moche were not sun worshipers like the Inca, but moon worshipers like the Chimu.

Recent scholars, among them Christopher Donnan and Elizabeth Benson, either dismissed the theory due to lack of evidence or avoided the entire question. Yet iconographic examples of the spiritual importance of the moon were plentiful, and circumstantial evidence suggested that the Moche may have used some form of lunar calendar. Furthermore, all of the artifacts that police seized from Ernil Bernal's house had been crafted to reflect some stage of a crescent or full moon.

Years earlier, Max Diaz had explained to the young Alva that, while the sun brought warmth and made agriculture possible in the otherwise cold and hostile mountains where the Incas originated, it was the enemy in the hot and arid desert, homeland of the Moche. Visible only at night and the early evening, the moon controlled the tides and fishing and carried cooling winds to the otherwise unbearable heat of the desert.

Almost all the stories that Mrs. Zapata and others told

Alva about the site contained references to depictions in Moche art that fell into three categories: supernatural creatures appearing to huaqueros in the process of looting; supernatural creatures appearing to huaqueros in narcotic-induced visions; and nocturnal animals and other creatures spying on or taking hold of villagers traveling on the road running between the Huaca Rajada pyramids.

In the most common of these stories, a pair of supernatural owls that nested in the tops of the two tallest pyramids caught hold of an innocent villager and carried him or her to their roost, where they proceeded to pluck out eyes or eat toes and fingers. The most recent of these stories was circulated after the half-eaten corpse of a teenage girl was found in an abandoned tunnel in 1974. Less superstitious residents of Sipan believed that the girl had committed suicide by throwing herself into the tunnel and had then been eaten by one of the animals that made its home there.

In support of her claim that huaqueros had uncovered ancient treasure at the site long before the appearance of Ernil and his men, Mrs. Zapata pointed out the remains of a clay kiln that she maintained had been used in the 1920s and 1930s to melt artifacts collected from the pyramids. A close examination indicated that the kiln had indeed been used to melt metal ornaments much like the basketful that Ricardo Zapata had unearthed.

Ricardo's ornaments, consisting of a hundred or more small copper links, may have been part of a chain-link jacket, or chain mail, similar to the kind of garment worn by a knight in medieval times. Like Ernil and his men, Ricardo had been in such a rush to pick his chamber clean that he couldn't be certain how the ornaments had been laid out, or exactly where and in what position they had been found.

In the days ahead, police investigators managed to retrieve ten more Moche artifacts from the homes of Ernil's associates, mostly through the keen detective work of Benedicto, who searched the field in back of the Bernal house and discovered another full rice sack, bringing the total number of individual pieces recovered from the Huaca Rajada looting operation to thirty-three. All these artifacts were clearly Moche, and most certainly from the tomb of a high-ranking individual. But in light of the number of pieces the police suspected were still on the black market, Alva believed that not all of them could reasonably have come out of the same royal burial chamber. He couldn't know for sure because there was no easy means of dating them. The ceramics that might have provided Alva a means of establishing an approximate period in Moche history in which they were made had been smashed beyond recognition. Bone samples, an accepted source for carbon dating, couldn't be used either because huaqueros and villagers had liberally scattered human and animal remains throughout the site.

For the time being, all Alva could say for certain about the "House of the Moon" was that Moche craftsmen had constructed at least one of the three giant pyramids, and that inside its platform the Moche had buried a monarch or lord and cut chambers that may have once housed a number of other burials, of greater or lesser importance.

Earlier, Alva had chosen not to take the police or Lucho into his confidence until he had time to think things through. Now he remained silent for other reasons. Either he had misunderstood the importance of the tomb or he had been mistaken about the very nature and ultimate purpose of the pyramid. Huaca Rajada, Alva speculated, might never have been a temple or ceremonial site like other Moche monuments on the north coast, or a mausoleum for one exalted lord and his trusted servants.

Huaca Rajada may have been an ancient necropolis for the lords of the Moche kingdom, the equivalent of the Egyptian Valley of the Kings, outside the city of Thebes.

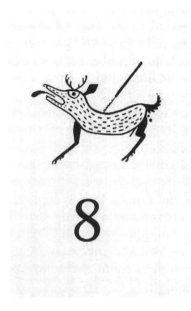

8

On April 3, after a month-long investigation of the looter's handiwork at Huaca Rajada, Alva hosted a press conference at police headquarters and later joined PIP investigators and a team of television reporters on a sunrise raid of the Bernal farmhouse.

In spite of the eagerness of the police to recover more Moche artifacts and the willingness of the press to cover the important events leading to their return, Alva had reservations about the success of another raid. Almost sixty-days had elapsed since Ernil and his men had looted the Moche burial chamber, more than enough time for them to put the artifacts on the black market in Lima. During that period the police had raided the homes of Ernil's brothers and suspected partners on three occasions. Though arrests had been made and several more looted Moche pieces seized, the artifacts that investigators had recovered amounted to little more than "gifts" in the form of gold beads and fragments of larger looted objects that

Ernil had presented to relatives and villagers. Nor had the raids shed any new light on the secrets of the plundered tomb or the location of the remaining artifacts. Instead of easing tensions at the site, they had stirred considerable resentment against police and archaeologists.

Nevertheless, the police had built a strong case against the huaqueros, the press had rallied to their side, and the sooner Ernil and his men stood behind bars, the more time Alva could devote to his research. Each hour Ernil remained at large, the more exaggerated were the tales he spun at the local cantina about golden treasures ripe for the plucking in the pyramid's platform, thereby making it increasingly hard for Alva and the police to slow the parade of huaqueros and poor villagers to the site. In the minds of local residents, Ernil had become a hero to be emulated, something of a Robin Hood of Huaca Rajada. "El Chino," as villagers called him, stole from the rich and gave to the poor, using his cunning and skill to stay one step ahead of the authorities trying to imprison him.

"I am the voice of the poor," he told a reporter from Chiclayo at the local cantina. "The treasures of Huaca Rajada are the treasures of our ancestors. They belong to us."

To compound Alva's apprehensions, the final raid kept being postponed because the press crews were not available at the same time that the police had the manpower and transportation to launch their offensive. By April 11, at five A.M., less than thirty-six hours before the scheduled premiere of an hour-long report on Huaca Rajada to be aired on a popular national television magazine show called *Panorama*, Alva still wasn't sure that the raid would take place.

Because of unforeseen complications at the museum, Alva arrived a half hour late at police headquarters. A team of nine policemen, all unfamiliar to him, sat in the back of a troop transport holding automatic weapons, looking more like an assault team than a police unit enforcing an arrest warrant. Unable to recruit the "elite" officers believed to be necessary for television cameras, Mondragon had enlisted a crack drug-interdiction force en route to a cocaine seizure at one of the nearby ports. Had Alva not been late and the press not so eager to leave, he might have protested the change and requested that Mondragon employ his regular officers. But as it was, Alva answered press questions, invited Panorama television host Alejandro Guerrero and his cameraman into the museum van, and took his place in the rear of a police motorcade.

When the police arrived at the Bernal farmhouse, they pulled up across from an irrigation canal, killed their lights, and remained inside their cars. Benedicto, driving the museum van that brought Alva and the television crew, also killed his lights. At the request of Guerrero, Temoche was to hold his men back until sunrise, when there would be enough light for Guerrero's cameraman to photograph the raid. However, five minutes after the police arrived, Ernil's father left the house to milk the cows and spotted the cars.

Members of Temoche's crack police unit caught and held Carlos Bernal before he could return to the house to alert the others. But his shouts startled the Bernal dog, asleep beside the Bernals' front door. Barking brought Ernil's mother, Eloisa, to the door. At the same time, two figures hidden in the shadows ran from the bedroom adjoining the side of the house and along the courtyard heading toward the sugarcane fields.

Five minutes later, one of Temoche's men came to the side of the museum van and told Alva and Guerrero what had happened. Ernil, in jeans and a torn blue T-shirt, had been arrested along with two others. In the process, the Bernal family dog had been shot, Ernil's older brother Juan grazed by a bullet, and Ernil wounded while attempting to escape.

"A success," the policeman told Alva and the reporters inside the museum van.

Except for the shooting, Alva had to concur. Ernil's arrest would finally put a halt to the stories he told the villagers, and without a leader to rally around, the huaqueros would migrate to other, less volatile archaeological sites. And though the Panorama cameraman had been unable to photograph the police action, Alejandro Guerrero had an ending for his story and the police had made their first important arrests in the looting investigation. Another search of the farmhouse was also under way, this time with a metal detector that police had confiscated from a pair of British tourists found trespassing at El Purgatorio, an archaeological site farther north.

Even though he had been shot in the back, Ernil didn't seem to be in pain or troubled. He looked, as Alva told reporters, "almost relieved." In truth, however, Alva didn't see Ernil for more than a moment or two because police commandeered Benedicto and the museum van to take Ernil and one of the policemen to the hospital in Chiclayo. And though Ernil may have looked relieved, Benedicto noticed how troubled Alva was. In the eight years he had worked for Alva, as driver, handyman, camp cook, auto mechanic, and bodyguard, Benedicto had rarely seen Alva so emotionally charged.

Like others at the Bruning, Benedicto understood that as much as Alva abhorred the activities of huaqueros, he also realized the economic conditions that caused poor villagers to loot ancient sites. From their point of view, if they didn't remove an artifact from the ground, someone else would. If they took the artifact to a police station or museum, chances are they would be accused of looting or stealing and thrown in jail. Besides, to their way of thinking, no one would miss an antiquity that was buried in the ground in the first place.

Alva had as great a distaste for the self-serving interests of the journalists covering the story as he had for the holier-than-thou attitude of many of his colleagues. For all their lip service, archaeologists were often no better than the looters themselves. The findings of only half of the sites excavated were ever published, and precious research was often left to rot or collect dust in museum basements. Under these circumstances, the artifacts themselves were as good as destroyed.

Until now, not one raid during Alva's ten-year campaign to protect the monuments under his supervision had resulted in a shooting. Shots may have been fired and people may have been hit by stones and bottles, but there had never been a serious injury. Nor had there been a television crew in the museum van and a chief of police put in charge of a crack team of armed officers. Everyone had gotten carried away, out of control. Ernil, father of two children of the same ages as Alva's Nacho and Bruno, could have been killed. As it was, his blood now permanently stained the upholstery in the Bruning van.

The deeply troubled Alva politely declined more interviews, excused himself, and walked to Huaca Rajada.

Upon his arrival about thirty minutes later, Alva did not return to the pyramid platform and his tent camp. Instead, he chose a separate trail along a rutted serpentine path of crumbling clay bricks set at a dizzying, nearly vertical uplift that ended at the top of the tallest of the three pyramids.

As Alva climbed the trail, he realized that for all the hours he had spent at the site, not once had he hiked to the top of the middle pyramid, the most beautiful place from which to see the rising sun cast its first rays of pastel light across the sugarcane fields. Perched atop a clay-brick pedestal at the pyramid's summit, Alva packed tobacco into a pipe that Max Diaz had given him and looked out at the lush green fields and the sun-baked brown rectangle of clay bricks far beneath him, across the horizon, past the twin blue-green hills known as the Dos Tetas, or "Twin Tits," then beyond, to the snow-covered foothills of the Andes. He would return to this spot so often in the coming days that superstitious villagers came to believe that he was conducting a ritual pago to the ancestral spirits of the "House of the Moon."

As he looked to the east, toward the sunken road that led to the ancient Moche ruins at Pampa Grande, it occurred to Alva that if his hypothesis about Huaca Rajada was correct—that the looted pyramid platform had once been a royal burial place for lords of the Moche kingdom—then there was a chance, however slim, that other royal burials at the site had been overlooked by huaqueros. And assuming that Ernil had been removed as a source of potential trouble and the museum raised the necessary funds, Alva and the Bruning could begin a full-scale excavation.

As Alva smoked his pipe and gazed off into the distance, he heard a horn honk. Below him, Benedicto was standing beside the museum van waving his arms and Lucho was running up the path toward the pyramid.

"It's Ernil," Lucho said, out of breath, as he reached Alva. "He died before surgeons could operate."

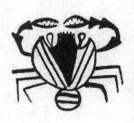

9

Ernil's "murder," as the villagers called the police action, couldn't have come at a more advantageous time for Fred Drew, the man whose crutches Enrico Poli had spotted in Pereda's kitchen. A retired diplomat, Drew was the principal player in the mass exodus of looted Moche artifacts out of Peru and onto the international black market; but he cultivated the image of an aging adventurer and scholar, more in the spirit of a nineteenth-century British explorer than a dealer in illegal exports.

Like his counterparts in the Lima black market, Drew was unknown to the general public, had no gallery, never advertised, and sold only to a select clientele. For the right price he could obtain practically anything, from a two-thousand-year-old ceramic burial urn for a London collector to a rare Peruvian blue-green hawk-headed parrot for a Japanese businessman.

Drew's interest in antiquities had begun on Cape Cod, Massachusetts, where he hunted for spear points, arrowheads, and stone effigies in old Indian cemeteries.

Later, stationed at the United States Embassy in Lima in the 1960s, Drew hired huaqueros to take him on prospecting trips to north-coast cemeteries and monuments. His personal collection of ceramics caught the attention of associates, and he soon became an unofficial travel agent and chaperone to foreign-service and military officers seeking souvenirs to bring home. As the value of ceramics increased in the late 1970s, Drew's "cottage industry" evolved into a full-time business that employed dozens of runners carrying looted artifacts from remote north-coast sites to his sumptuous Art Deco home across the street from Lima's most loved public park.

By Drew's own admission, he paid little attention to the 1929 laws banning the plunder of graves and exportation of antiquities. To him, corruption had long been endemic throughout Peruvian society; and his monthly excursions to remote archaeological sites not only provided much needed money to a depressed region but also helped to further knowledge and interest in the ancient Peruvian cultures. Moreover, he believed that archaeologists and police officials overlooked the dedication of the serious dealer, his specialized scholarship and authentic commitment to art. Nor were endowments sufficient to care for all the antiquities already in public collections. Each year, Peruvian curators reported more and more gold objects missing from their collections, and precious textiles were left to rot in subterranean basements because government agencies hadn't the money, skills, or technology to care for them. According to Drew, Alva's predecessor at the Bruning had once offered to let him select up to ten pieces at bargain prices from among the museum's finest pottery specimens, intending to declare the pieces "lost" in an earthquake.

With a vast working knowledge of the intricacies of his adopted nation's business practices and a virtual pipeline to the north-coast huaqueros, Drew earned a reputation as a solid and reliable businessman whose client list included European heads of state and major United States and English museums. And just as he was reaching the high point of his twenty-year career in the trade, the treasures of Huaca Rajada provided him with a retirement opportunity he hadn't previously believed possible. He now could imagine himself well ensconced in a villa on the green rolling hills in the highlands above Trujillo, surrounded by *viringos*, the hairless Peruvian dogs he bred for profit and companionship.

To turn that retirement plan into a reality, however, Drew had had to take on a secret partner in the United States, someone in a position to help him raise the $80,000 he needed to purchase the first shipment of Huaca Rajada treasures and then to furnish the additional $225,000 he needed to place orders, sight unseen, for the rest. Each morning for the past month or more, so it seemed to Drew, this secret partner sent him another DHL overseas express-mail package containing cashier's checks payable to Drew in amounts of $9,999, just under the $10,000 limit that banks must report to international-tax and customs inspectors. No sooner had he cashed the checks than runners arrived bearing more Moche treasures. After making the initial purchase, Drew didn't even have to leave home.

But now that television reporters and the press had photographed Ernil's funeral cortege marching past the Huaca Rajada pyramids, the entire situation changed. Because buyers liked "hot pieces" that had a "colorful past," the media exposure meant that Drew's partner could extract almost ten times the original purchase price.

Normally, Drew preferred not to conduct business out of his house. He met clients and associates at restaurants or their hotel rooms and asked that his alias, "Don Paredes," be used in all letters and telephone conversations. Even then, he seldom brought looted goods or illegal merchandise to a meeting, but had a courier deliver them to a mutually agreeable location at a later date. More often than not, Drew carried only Polaroid photographs of his most valuable objects. But because of the long-term relationship he and his partner had developed and the large amounts of cash and merchandise involved, Drew made an exception for the Huaca Rajada treasures and agreed to supervise the transfer of the first shipment himself.

In the past, Drew had used tourists, airplane personnel, and even nuns to carry his antiquities from Lima to the United States. When his business developed into a full-time occupation, he began shipping ceramic pieces overland to La Paz, the capital of Bolivia, where customs officials were much more relaxed about the transshipment of goods received over its borders. Drew would then have mud slips painted onto the bottoms of the pots and stamp them "Hecho en Bolivia," or "Made in Bolivia," before sending them to Vancouver to be driven across the border into the United States.

Until recently, Drew and his partner had used this method to ship a hundred or more pre-Columbian ceramics to clients in Arizona and New Mexico. But problems arose in 1985 when Vancouver customs agents, suspecting narcotics shipments, inspected two ceramic and textile consignments. A third shipment might have been Drew's undoing had he not stopped it in La Paz.

Because of the increased risk of moving valuable artifacts in large quantities, Drew's partner decided to limit Drew's responsibilities to procurement and devised an entirely new shipping route out of Peru to London and from London into the United States. Drew's risk in their operation ended the moment he put the Moche treasures in the hands of Miguel de Osma Berckemeyer, Lima's notorious "export agent" and "problem solver."

To the uninitiated, Berckemeyer appeared to be little more than a young Lima playboy living on a generous family allowance. Nephew of the former Peruvian ambassador to the United States and member of one of the most important banking families in the nation, Berckemeyer spent his leisure time jetting between the roulette tables in Rio and the mansions of Hollywood film producers. Here the resemblance to the idle young rich stopped, because the thirty-three-year-old Berckemeyer had little interest in taking charge of the family fortune, nor had his family any intention of passing it on to him. Berckemeyer thought of himself as Lima's most influential "expediter." By his own admission he used his family connections and contacts in the Medellin drug cartel to operate a private import and export service, boasting to clients that he could have suitcases ushered through customs without being opened; conversely, he could also have them seized and searched. Not even his associates knew the full extent of his influence, but all recognized the special services he could render, especially Drew. Ironically, it was one of Berckemeyer's cash-rich friends in Medellin who had become Drew's only real competition in the quest for the remaining Huaca Rajada treasures.

By mutual agreement, Drew received expenses plus 22.5 percent of the profits from the sale of Huaca Rajada artifacts and any other antiquities that he turned over to Berckemeyer. In return for 5 percent of the total value of each shipment, Berckemeyer handled customs clearance in Lima en route to London, keeping 50 percent of that fee while the other half went to his contacts at the airport. For security reasons, neither Drew nor Berckemeyer knew how Drew's partner planned to move the shipments into the United States, the last and most precarious leg of their journey from Huaca Rajada.

In the aftermath of Ernil's slaying, Berckemeyer telephoned Drew from a pay phone on the street before approaching the back entrance to Drew's town house. As he had on previous meetings, Berckemeyer left his two private guards in his car, knocked on the door, then followed Drew's private attendant through the kitchen and living room to Drew's private cedar-paneled office.

In his customary gentlemanly manner, Drew attempted to engage Berckemeyer in conversation about the archaeological significance of the Moche artifacts and the latest developments at Huaca Rajada. Police informants in Chiclayo and Lima had told Drew that public outrage over Ernil's death had resulted in an unofficial end to the Huaca Rajada investigation, and that Alva and his assistant planned to abandon the site. Unable to obtain more Moche tomb ornaments from his contacts in Lima and Trujillo, Enrico Poli had traveled to Chiclayo and Lambayeque to stir up resentment against the police and to try to purchase any artifacts still in the hands of the remaining Bernal brothers. But Drew no longer considered Poli a threat. Except for Berckemeyer's friend in Medellin, whose antiquities collection he knew nothing about, Drew and his partner had cornered the international market.

In Berckemeyer, Drew sensed an impatience with scholarship, an outright irritation with ponderous old men like himself. Talk of Huaca Rajada and the significance of the Moche ornaments bored him. As far as Berckemeyer was concerned, the Moche tomb ornaments could have been kilos of cocaine from the jungle, gold and emeralds from the mountains, or even antique furniture, the commodity that had brought Drew and Berckemeyer together less than a month earlier. Berckemeyer entered into the conversation only to mention the other services he could furnish for a slightly higher percentage of the total shipment. Among these services was the armed protection of the pieces to their ultimate destinations in Europe and the United States, and the "removal" of any individuals who might cause problems.

Drew preferred not to hear anything more about these services because he still considered himself blameless in his role in the antiquities trade. Berckemeyer might not appreciate such subtleties, but Drew's partner and his partner's clients in Europe and the United States represented scholars, museum officials, and leaders in their respective fields.

Before the conversation could continue, Drew signaled his personal attendant to enter the secured storeroom off the kitchen and retrieve the Moche ornaments that composed the Berckemeyer shipment. The attendant soon returned carrying the individual pieces in an open shipping crate. Each piece was wrapped in brown paper, packed in roasted peanuts, and individually logged on an inventory list that Drew placed on the table for Berckemeyer to inspect. Later, under separate cover, a signed copy of this document would be forwarded to Drew's partner.

As always, Berckemeyer showed no real interest in the contents of the shipment. He counted all twenty-five items to be placed in his care but, like a bored customs agent, examined only one or two before accepting Drew's inventory at face value. According to that inventory, the total value of the shipment amounted to approximately $60,000, about the price of one kilo of processed cocaine at its source. Based on Berckemeyer's transportation agreement, he and his contact in customs split $3,000. Drew failed to mention that because of Ernil's shooting the value of this particular shipment now amounted to closer to $150,000.

Ten minutes after he arrived, Berckemeyer closed the lid on the crate, Drew's attendant nailed it shut, then

Berckemeyer carried it out the back entrance. Berckemeyer's two men took the crate, locked it into the trunk of the parked car, and joined Berckemeyer for the twenty-five-minute trip to the cargo terminal at the Lima airport. By previous arrangement, the antiquities would be loaded onto a plane bound for London.

Later, when interviewed by a reporter, Drew would remember watching Berckemeyer's car pull into the late-afternoon traffic and wondering what the ancient Moche might have thought about the plane trip. To this question, Drew had no answer, but one thing was certain: At no time since their creation had these artifacts traveled so fast and so far from their home.

PART 3

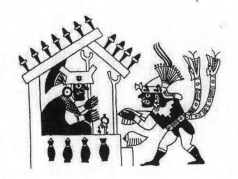

TEMPLE OF THE FANGED DEITY

10

Like the rest of the Bruning personnel, Lucho knew that the stakes had changed at Huaca Rajada. Each hour, more villagers rallied together in Ernil's name and paraded past the archaeological tent camp to proclaim police injustice and call for the immediate expulsion of the "thieves" and "murderers" from the sacred Moche monument. Thus, on the morning of April 13, 1987, Lucho was relieved when Alva asked the police to clear the site and requested to be taken to the corporate boardroom of the Napoli Noodle Company in Chiclayo, where he was to meet a committee of museum sponsors. Here, Lucho assumed that Alva planned to announce his evacuation of the site and raise the cash he needed to hire men and equipment to seal the pyramid platform.

To Lucho's horror, Alva proposed an alternative plan to Giorgio Batastini of Napoli Noodles, German Gorbitz of the Northern Beer Company, and Fernando Guillen, a prominent physician in Chiclayo. "I'm not leaving Huaca Rajada," Alva told the museum sponsors. "I'm going to excavate."

Stunned at the announcement, Lucho couldn't bring himself to respond until their trip back to the museum. Even then, he couldn't excuse the casual, last-minute approach Alva had taken to inform him of his intentions. "It's one thing to put your own life on the line," Lucho told Alva. "It's another to expect me to join you."

In the three years and four months that Lucho had assisted Alva at the Bruning, he had never openly voiced his disapproval of anything Alva planned, nor had he even considered handing in his resignation. Although he sometimes found his employer unpredictable and overly secretive, Lucho's tenure at the museum had been the most exciting and instructive period in his life, made all the richer because of Alva's staunch support of Lucho's promotion to the rank of supervising archaeologist and his resolute commitment that the INC appoint Lucho to a position equal to his impressive talents. Not that Alva hadn't made Lucho's apprenticeship hard.

Lucho had first introduced himself to Alva on a summer- vacation visit to the museum. In the course of a casual conversation, Lucho mentioned the lack of hands-on field experience he had received as a graduate student at the University of Trujillo in the same archaeological program Alva had attended. Two hours later, Lucho stood holding a spade in one hand and a brush in the other, about to assist Alva in the excavation of a prehistoric burial mound near El Purgatorio. Except for a short trip back to the University of Trujillo to collect his credentials as an archaeologist, Lucho remained at Alva's side through months of labor under the scorching sun and sleepless nights on rain-soaked blankets in remote jungle campsites. Following the lead that Alva himself set, Lucho surrendered a portion of his meager income to help preserve and excavate sites that might otherwise have been left to huaqueros. He slept on a cot in a rear storeroom at the museum, ate meals at Alva's house in the museum courtyard, and spent his free time helping to repair or replace archaeological tools.

Huaca Rajada had now come between them, a subject that became the main topic of conversation on their return trip from Napoli Noodles. That night, in the museum basement, Lucho announced he would accept the new INC position regardless of the crisis at Huaca Rajada.

Lucho had no intention of attempting to talk Alva into a reappraisal of the potential archaeological significance of the site. Fellow experts in pre-Inca cultures seldom questioned Alva's expertise, primarily because Alva had more experience excavating a broader variety of field sites than any other living archaeologist in Peru, perhaps more than anyone on the entire continent. Even if he operated on his own agenda and his theories sometimes ran contrary to popular opinion, Alva's hunches almost always brought immediate results.

Instead of arguing about the archaeological potential of Huaca Rajada, Lucho cited the trouble Mrs. Zapata had encountered during Ernil's funeral. An estimated 175 people had turned out for the April 12 event, marching slowly from the Bernal house through the village of Sipan and then past Huaca Rajada on their way to the contemporary cemetery, about a half-mile south of the site. According to police, the huaqueros placed an apron made of looted Huaca Rajada gold across Ernil's body before lowering his corpse into the grave. Upon this apron, each huaquero allegedly inscribed his name, vowing to avenge his killing. Mercedes Zapata became one of their first targets.

Huaqueros claimed that they had pelted Mrs. Zapata

and her son with stones because she had insulted the Bernal family by wearing a red dress on the morning of Ernil's funeral. Police, on the other hand, maintained that the attack had been prompted by Mrs. Zapata's cooperation with investigators, and that, although she had had a red dress on at the time of the funeral, Mrs. Zapata hadn't insulted the Bernals because she hadn't attended the service.

Lucho pointed out that it would not be long before the same gang of huaqueros, stirred into action by the sight of archaeologists at Huaca Rajada, sought retribution on Alva. And after public criticism for the police handling of the Bernal investigation, pressure from above had forced Temoche and Mondragon to reconsider their previous commitment to provide Lucho and Alva with armed protection. Before the end of the month the police might not even be a presence at the site.

Not only would excavating at Huaca Rajada be dangerous, Lucho pointed out, it would be expensive. Napoli Noodles, the Northern Beer Company, and other museum sponsors had raised approximately three hundred dollars in cash and an additional one hundred dollars in equipment, cases of beer, clothing, and cartons of pasta noodles. Such meager essentials might be a start toward excavating the huaqueros' tunnels; but the Bruning hadn't the additional cash reserves to complete the job, which would leave the site in an even more vulnerable and exposed position. Far better, Lucho believed, to use sponsors' cash to heap tons of sand and soil onto the top of the platform than to remove the remaining top layer of hardened adobe bricks and then abandon the pyramid to the huaqueros.

Lucho stated his case in a succinct and organized manner, careful not to vent his frustration at not being told of Alva's plans earlier or to say that the Moche had never held the same fascination for him as they had for Alva. But rather than respond to Lucho's concerns one at a time, as Lucho expected, Alva paternally put his arm over Lucho's shoulder and counseled him not to resign until the situation became more clear. Regarding their financial position, Alva told him that as soon as the excavation began, he expected that sheer momentum and enthusiasm would carry their project to its completion. And once it was clear that the archaeologists had not come to Huaca Rajada to steal or plunder but to conduct a scientific excavation, the villagers and huaqueros would become bored and lose interest in their presence.

Frustrated in his attempt to open a more productive line of communication, Lucho sought the council of Alva's wife, Susana, the one person he believed he could count on to intercede on his behalf. But instead of coming to his rescue, Susana endorsed her husband's plans to excavate. In so doing she provided Lucho with a rare glimpse into the otherwise private relationship between her and Alva.

Upon her return from Trujillo and throughout her husband's month-long self-imposed exile at the site, Susana Alva had chosen to keep silent on the subject of Huaca Rajada. As a fellow archaeologist, she shared her husband's interests; provided that he take his bronchitis medication and inform her and the police of his movements, she gave her tacit approval to whatever he was doing. Like Lucho she had believed that once police arrested Ernil and exposed his contacts in the Trujillo and Lima black markets, Huaca Rajada would cease to be the target of antipolice sentiment. Ernil's shooting had changed all that for Lucho and Alva as it had for her. But for different reasons. Unknown to Lucho, two visitors had made secret trips to the museum to talk to Susana, each bearing news or information that substantially altered how she and her husband had come to view the crisis.

Esmilda Bernal, the mother of Ernil's orphaned children, arrived at the museum just before closing time on April 13. A plump, large-boned woman, Esmilda waited on the rear steps at the museum's exit until the security patrolman had gone into the exhibition hall to turn out the lights. As the patrolman left, Esmilda sprinted across the courtyard and hid in an alley adjacent to the Alva home, just behind the administrative offices. Susana noticed Esmilda there an hour later. A small solid- gold Moche tomb ornament that Esmilda was carrying served as the only introduction she needed.

Susana soon realized the enormous risk Esmilda had taken in coming to see her. Ernil's brothers, apparently unable to restrain their greed, had made plans to cut Esmilda and her children out of Ernil's share of the looted artifacts. Fearing more police seizures and shootings on one hand and the wrath of Ernil's brothers on the other, Esmilda sought to trade information and antiquities for cash and protection. In return for five thousand dollars, an amount she later reduced to one thousand dollars, Esmilda offered to sell Alva and police investigators the remaining Moche treasures and to reveal the names of her late husband's contacts in the Trujillo and Lima black markets. With the money she received, she planned to make a new life for herself and her children elsewhere.

Esmilda's offer caused an instant sensation among police officials eager to put the now unpopular investigation behind them. In return for the one thousand dollars paid to Esmilda, a portion of which Alva had already raised through museum sponsors, police investigators could arrest all the suspects and seize the remaining Moche treasures. Doing so, however, meant breaking a rule that Alva considered sacred—that neither he nor anyone in his employ would purchase artifacts from collectors or trade in looted antiquities. Attractive as the offer was, Susana had to tell Esmilda no. To act otherwise would be endorsing the very criminal behavior Alva campaigned to stop.

Ironically, investigators knew that just one of the more valuable looted Moche pieces in Esmilda's possession, if sold to a man like Poli, could raise enough money for Alva to pay Esmilda, hire round-the-clock security at the site, and still have enough funds left over to excavate Huaca Rajada. And no matter how high Alva's ethical standards, this thought must have crossed Susana's mind when the second of her two visitors arrived at the museum.

As a practical matter, Enrico Poli took a professional interest in the important pre-Inca collections at the Bruning. On every trip he took to Lambayeque, he stopped in to see any new items that had been added and to compare his own gold and silver pieces to those on exhibit in the high-security vault room. On this trip, however, he wanted to look at the artifacts that had been seized in the police raid and to pass along a message on behalf of so-called "contacts" he claimed to represent among north-coast antiquity traders. According to Poli, these contacts had hatched a plot to have Alva assassinated should he move ahead with his plans to excavate.

Susana never asked Poli how he knew that her husband planned to go ahead and excavate, but she suspected that the same contacts who had a vested interest in Huaca Rajada also had spies among the ranks of museum sponsors or the police. Regardless of the source of his information, however, Poli made his message clear, and his formidable reputation in the Peruvian underworld removed any doubt that he was making an idle threat. Either Alva withdrew from the site or his enemies would send an assassin to kill him.

Poli clearly knew pre-Inca antiquities better than he

knew Susana Alva and her relationship with her husband. In their often tempestuous thirteen-year marriage, she and Alva had disagreed about practically everything from environmental politics to money management. But not once had she asked him to compromise an archaeological project for her sake. Ever since they had chosen to take their honeymoon at a remote jungle excavation, archaeology had been a passion that could not be denied. Their children had learned to exchange a sandbox for an excavation pit, and weekend trips to Lima were routinely passed up for a quiet family picnic collecting fossils.

Poli clearly intended to frighten Susana as a wife and mother, but he succeeded only in angering her as an archaeologist. Infuriated, she launched into a verbal tirade that caught the attention of everyone at the Bruning, and Benedicto had to remove Poli from the museum before she lost complete control over her emotions. "No thief is going to tell me how to run an excavation," she shouted at him. "It's that simple. If you kill Walter, then I'll take his place. And if you kill me, then there'll be someone else to take my place."

This talk of assassination plots convinced Lucho once and for all that he had no alternative except to leave the museum before real trouble began. On the morning of April 14, less than a day after Alva had publicly made the decision to excavate, Lucho once again requested that Alva sign his transfer papers. Alva surprised Lucho by having the papers in his jacket pocket, signed.

Prior to handing the papers to Lucho, however, Alva extracted a last promise. In return for Alva's help in getting Lucho settled in his new position in Cajamarca, or "outside of the cross fire," as Alva put it, Lucho would agree to remain in his present position until the end of the month. Lucho, estimating that Alva needed that time to catch up on museum business, lay out his plans for the site, purchase supplies, and petition INC superiors in Lima for a permit to excavate, agreed.

11

How Alva managed to acquire an excavation permit in less time than it took most archaeologists to complete the INC application was a question that puzzled Lucho. Alva surrendered no budget to his superiors in Lima, outlined none of his excavation plans on paper, or, to Lucho's knowledge, placed one phone call to his contacts at INC headquarters. All Lucho knew for certain was that on April 14, as Ernil's partners and other villagers joined together to unveil a carved black-marble stone memorial to "El Chino," their fallen hero, Alva cashed his sponsors' checks, purchased building supplies, and arranged for a police escort to take him and Lucho back to Huaca Rajada.

Lucho hadn't received an explanation about the excavation permit because Alva never obtained one. In the first of a long series of bold and controversial moves calculated to keep one step ahead of his critics, Alva used his position as the INC's regional supervisor to classify his activities at Huaca Rajada as a "salvage operation" designed to repair the looted platform. Although Alva's INC position permitted him to make such a judgment, not one visitor to the site over the next month and a half suspected Alva of running anything but a full-time excavation.

His real plans at Huaca Rajada, like those he had for Lucho, became clear when Alva raised the INC colors on a makeshift pole over the entrance to the site and proceeded to plant a grid of sharpened surveyor's stakes around the perimeter of the areas he intended to excavate first. Even though he had accepted Lucho's resignation, signed his transfer papers, and expressed his interest in using his professional contacts to see Lucho settled at another post, Alva made it next to impossible for Lucho to leave his side. Whenever Lucho proposed returning to the museum, Alva assigned him some new task that required his immediate attention in one of the looters' tunnels, or sent the museum van on an errand. And since the nearest telephone and radio communications were at a military base more than thirty miles away, Lucho had to rely on Alva to keep abreast of news from the INC.

Instead of posting a notice in the trade journals that he was seeking a replacement, Alva made an even bolder move than the one he had taken by coming to Huaca Rajada. In spite of his meager, almost nonexistent cash reserves, Alva informed friends and colleagues that he intended to hire a crew of ten additional excavators. Furthermore, he announced that he had no intention of hiring from the pool of trained personnel he had used on previous excavations but would employ villagers, regardless of their training or experience.

True to his promise, Alva shocked colleagues and villagers alike by hiring Marcial Montessa, a known huaquero, for the position of chief foreman. About his previous looting activities Alva had no doubt, because both he and Lucho had chased Montessa from other archaeological sites. In the course of the short interview Alva conducted, Montessa himself alluded to "visits" he had made to these sites, apparently trying to leave the impression that his experience somehow entitled him to the highest-paid position at Huaca Rajada besides that of chief excavator.

Alva hired the twenty-three-year-old Montessa for one important reason: Montessa was the first resident to challenge the local boycott. Prior to Montessa's arrival, Alva had spent an entire morning hiking from house to house in Sipan to introduce himself and inform residents of employment opportunities. But in spite of economic hardships in the area, mainly brought about by the failure of the Pomalca farm cooperative to issue paychecks for the last two months, residents closed their doors in Alva's face or told him to leave before Ernil's partners and older brothers made good on their much-vaunted promise to kill him. Early on the morning of April 16, however, before the usual crowd of protesters assembled at the entrance to Huaca Rajada, Montessa appeared in front of Alva's tent and asked for a job.

Virtually everyone else connected with the excavation, including Lucho, believed Alva had made a mistake by hiring a known huaquero for the position of chief foreman. Working on the pyramid platform would offer him temptation enough, but having him in a position of authority was asking to be robbed. At the very least, Lucho thought that Montessa would abandon excavators at a critical moment. And practically everyone at the site knew how soon that moment might come.

Alva, however, interpreted Montessa's employment at the site as a minor victory. Montessa knew the territory around Huaca Rajada as well as anyone did and could be expected to point out nearby sites that might have some archaeological bearing on the excavation. He indeed might act as a spy for the other huaqueros, but he could also act as a spy for the archaeologists, keeping Lucho and Alva apprised of developments in the village of Sipan, and of rumors circulating at the cantina. Alva readily admitted that Montessa's excavating techniques had to be altered to fit the exacting procedures required by the Bruning, but he was also young, clearly eager to learn the trade of an archaeologist, and, as a result of the years he had spent as a huaquero, had no fear of the tight, cramped crawlspaces under the pyramid platform. Nor had he fear of the hostile crowds that gathered just beyond the entrance to Huaca Rajada each morning and remained long into the night.

"Better to have him excavating the site in the daytime," Alva told Lucho, "than looting the site at night."

More significant in the long run, however, was Montessa's encouragement of others to follow his lead and cross the line of protesters. Two hours after Montessa accepted Alva's offer of three dollars a day plus meals, more job applicants appeared on the looted platform, first one at a time, then in pairs.

Armando Carrasco, a man Alva hired on Montessa's recommendation for $2.75 a day plus meals, had been a former field hand, laid off from the nearby farm cooperative the year before. Maximo Camacho, known as Max, and his friend Rosendo Dominguez, known as Domingo, were also itinerant farm workers who were willing to put up with the abuse and harassment of fellow villagers in return for $2.50 a day plus meals. Juan Martinez, a seventeen-year-old, hadn't known Montessa or any of the others, but had been inside the Bruning Museum and had demonstrated a genuine love for artifacts. Fernando Rojas, at age sixty-three, was the oldest laborer. Though nothing about his character indicated that he had the skills to become a first- class excavator, Alva considered his presence a bargain because he had the strength of two men.

Rojas and the others were hired as untrained day

laborers, a job so tortuous that most men preferred employment in the nearby sugarcane fields or at a local factory, if jobs could be obtained. At best, they would be required to haul tons of adobe brick and loose rubble when the thermometer hit 90 degrees by nine A.M. and there would be no decent breeze before three in the afternoon. Huaqueros tolerated these conditions because of the chance that their fortune lay just another shovelful away. But where huaqueros occasionally become rich, archaeological crew members received little more than encouragement and a regular paycheck, and in the case of Huaca Rajada, Alva couldn't guarantee either for very long.

Of all the available jobs, the one Alva had the most trouble filling was that of camp cook. It wasn't that Alva or his men were particular about their meals. After a long, hard day of work, they preferred quantity over quality. Alva's problem was logistical, since he hadn't outfitted the camp with anything besides a small kerosene stove and a few utensils. Without electricity or running water, an expansion of the present camp kitchen was out of the question.

Under normal circumstances Alva would have hired a local restaurant to cater their meals; but at Huaca Rajada, the closest thing to a restaurant consisted of the Sipan cantina, the hangout of Ernil's brothers and their friends. And even if there were another restaurant, no cook could be expected to cross the line of protesters that surrounded Huaca Rajada.

Mercedes Zapata came to Alva's rescue. Her kitchen, right at the foot of the looted platform, came complete with two large built-in stoves and enough space to sit the entire crew of thirteen in two shifts. Just behind her house, on the edge of the pyramid platform itself, she had a chicken coop and her now legendary rabbit hutch. Villagers already considered her an outcast, so she had nothing to lose and everything to gain. Becoming the camp cook not only brought her under the official protection of guards patrolling the site but helped to legitimize her claim of squatter's rights.

Mrs. Zapata and Alva struck a quick and highly unusual arrangement. In return for hiring her son Ricardo as one of the camp laborers, permission to remain on INC property, and the promise to put a new roof on her house, Mrs. Zapata agreed to purchase supplies and prepare meals for Alva and his crew.

This final task accomplished, excavation began on April 16, less than three days after Alva had made his urgent plea to museum sponsors in the boardroom of Napoli Noodles. Except for the crowds of twenty to thirty unemployed villagers that surrounded the site and the occasional bottle heaved at their tent, Alva seemed to have overcome all of his major obstacles except proper funding. On this point, Lucho's grim predictions proved most accurate. By hiring as many people as he had and paying out more than he intended on incidentals, Alva couldn't meet his daily payroll.

Three days into their excavation, Alva had already spent the three hundred dollars he had received from museum sponsors, along with the meager savings he had set aside for an expansion of the museum and the continuation of ongoing mapping and salvage projects. All obligations at Huaca Rajada now had to be paid in cases of Garza beer and cartons of Napoli Noodles.

In private communication with his associates in Lima, even Alva lost some of the enthusiasm and uncompromising optimism he had brought to the project.

"My excavation at Huaca Rajada," he wrote, "has ended before it began."

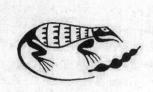

12

No one anticipated help to reach Huaca Rajada in time to prevent the exodus of Montessa and his men. But on April 20, 1987, two separate events heralded a rescue: the unexpected arrival of Moche scholar Christopher B. Donnan, and the startling discovery that huaqueros had overlooked a prize treasure in the looted burial chamber.

"Mr. Moche," as the press later characterized Donnan, arrived in Lima on April 17, on a spur-of-the-moment trip to expedite the processing of a permit for him and his students to excavate the following summer at Pacatnamu, in the Jequetepeque Valley. Between visits to INC officials, Donnan telephoned Alva at the Bruning Museum to inform him about some extraordinary Moche artifacts that he had recently examined and photographed in the homes of private collectors and dealers in Lima and Trujillo. Alva told Donnan that not only had he heard about the artifacts, but Chiclayo police had seized even more before they reached the black market. In addition, he had begun to excavate the tomb from which they had been looted. At Alva's invitation, Donnan agreed to come to the

Bruning to examine the artifacts seized by police and then to visit Huaca Rajada.

Alva couldn't believe his good fortune in having a man of Donnan's stature and influence in the archaeological community call at such a critical moment. Ever since they had first met, more than ten years earlier, Donnan had helped support Alva's work at the Bruning as Alva had supported Donnan's research at UCLA. At that time, the summer of 1976, Donnan had already spent five years traveling Europe in a Volkswagen van, and then another three years traveling the Americas, all the while photographing and examining the important private and public collections of Moche antiquities for inclusion in his Moche Archive at UCLA. By then, Alva had studied the two books that Donnan had written on the Moche, so his reputation had preceded him when Donnan arrived at the museum and introduced himself to Alva, then the assistant director, and asked if he could photograph the Bruning's collection. Because of their mutual interests and fondness for Moche iconography, a close friendship emerged, made closer by a friendship between their children, Matt Donnan, aged seven, and Nacho Alva, aged six.

News of Donnan's imminent arrival at Huaca Rajada was soon overshadowed by a discovery that Montessa and his men made while cleaning loose adobe brick and sand from inside the looted burial chamber. Montessa was on his hands and knees when his trowel revealed a niche that had been cut into the adobe bricks in the northwest corner of the chamber. Under Lucho and Alva's direction, Montessa kept digging until it was clear that huaqueros had overlooked a large object embedded in the wall, a three-foot-long copper scepter. When Alva freed it, he beheld a haunting scene sculptured in miniature on its head: a supernatural creature, half-feline and half-reptile, copulating with a woman upon a throne canopied by a peaked roof. Double rows of mace heads formed a balustrade around the throne, just as the knights of King Arthur's Round Table may have once hung shields on the backs of their chairs. Above the ridge line of the roof, seventeen tiny double-faced human heads were each crowned with a horned helmet.

The discovery of the scepter so excited Alva that he could barely pull himself away long enough to pick Donnan up at the airport. Not only was the leading expert in Moche art and iconography on his way to Huaca Rajada, but Alva had something to show him that few archaeologists in the world could appreciate: an object that cast new light on one of the most obscure and mysterious aspects of the Moche culture.

Less than two hours after Donnan's call, Alva met the forty-seven-year-old UCLA professor as he stepped off the Faucett Airlines commuter flight into the late-afternoon heat in the large, open-air passenger terminal at the Chiclayo airport. Donnan, a handsome, unassuming bearded man with closely cropped blond hair and brown eyes, carried Nikon cameras and a passport that had been stamped so many times, he could have been taken for a tourist on a round-the-world excursion. Benedicto helped Donnan into the Bruning's Volkswagen van, charged the engine, and took him and Alva back to the museum.

Alva used the hour ride to apprise Donnan of the events that had transpired since Alva had been called to police headquarters three months earlier. He saw no need to dwell on the perilous situation between the archaeologists and the villagers, nor would the telling have mattered. Less than a year before, Donnan himself had been in an even more dangerous situation when his wife, son, several graduate students, and assorted visitors and workers were assaulted by five men with guns who arrived in a truck at their Pacatnamu base camp. Realizing how grave their situation was, Donnan held the bandits off with a pistol he kept in his backpack until help arrived. Even though the ensuing shoot-out effectively ended excavation at Pacatnamu that summer, the experience hadn't dampened Donnan's eagerness to probe the secrets of the Moche.

Without even pausing to show Donnan the major improvements at the Bruning, Alva escorted his colleague past the administrative offices and through the foot-thick steel vault door into the rear wing to see the artifacts that the police had seized during their raids on the Bernal farmhouse and the homes of Ernil's associates. Here, in the "gold room," as frequent visitors called this section of the museum, Alva placed the artifacts on the examination table in the same position he believed priests may have dressed the corpse of a Moche lord before burial.

Laid out in this fashion—the moon-shaped masks, nose rings, and circular ear spools at the head, the necklaces of polished beads and sheet gold below them—the artifacts shone with a radiance all the more impressive than when Alva had first viewed them at police headquarters. Now meticulously cleaned, scraped, and polished by the museum staff, every object looked as if it had emerged only the day before from the bench of a Moche craftsman.

Donnan had the same startled reaction to the plundered treasures that Alva had had. But, unlike Alva, Donnan was reluctant to ascribe the antiquities to the burial of an important Moche lord, or even two lords. Donnan, who had examined ten or twelve looted artifacts in Enrico Poli's collection and an equal number at the home of Fred Drew, believed the antiquities to be less the personal possessions of one individual than the relics from a Moche religious ceremony.

Making no secret of his reluctance to ascribe the

artifacts to a burial, Donnan urged Alva to compare the motifs, or imagery, that appeared on them to the iconographic depictions of the sacrifice ceremony, a horrific Moche ritual that consisted of taking blood from captured prisoners and presenting it in a goblet to the Moche lord. Alva had only to examine the photographs that Donnan had taken in the homes of collectors, and to consult his heavily underlined edition of Moche Art of Peru, to see Donnan's point.

Among the artifacts in Enrico Poli's collection was a goblet identical to the one depicted in the sacrifice ceremony being handed to the Moche lord. The lord depicted in this ceremony also had ear ornaments, a crescent-shaped nose ring, and a back flap identical to the artifacts laid out on the examination table. Donnan also had a photograph of the jaguar head that Fred Drew had purchased. In all likelihood, it was never meant to be a figurine at all, but the centerpiece of a headdress. A similar headdress ornament was also depicted in the sacrifice ceremony. Drew hadn't recognized the artifact as part of a headdress because huaqueros had discarded its leather mounting and backing in the mistaken belief that anything not made of gold or silver wasn't worth saving.

Donnan's suggestion of a direct relationship between artifacts from Huaca Rajada and the sacrifice ceremony proved to be quite prophetic. But his remarks that afternoon hadn't the same resonance that they would assume when Donnan's contacts took delivery of enough looted artifacts for him to realize that royal tombs at Huaca Rajada contained both the relics of the sacrifice ceremony and the personal possessions of a monarch. A Moche lord's uniform in death, Donnan learned, reflected his responsibilities in life.

Donnan pointed out another parallel between Moche iconography and actual artifacts when Benedicto drove him and Alva to Huaca Rajada to examine the copper scepter. Tiny green roof tiles used to decorate the scepter looked identical to fragments of larger clay tiles that Montessa had excavated from around the entrance to the looted burial chambers. Based partially on this evidence and on other depictions in Moche art, Donnan confirmed Alva's suspicion that a throne similar to the one depicted on the scepter had once festooned Huaca Rajada.

Like Alva, Donnan instantly recognized the creature depicted on the scepter as the supreme Moche spirit in his most fearsome incarnation: half-feline and half-reptile. Because of severe deterioration of the modeled copper, neither Alva nor Donnan could say exactly where the feline left off and the reptile began, but the basic outline was clear. Mouth opened, claws extended, the Fanged Deity of the scepter had the human pinned to its throne, plunging its penis deep between the victim's spread legs.

Erotic depictions similar to the one portrayed on the scepter had led many archaeologists to believe that the Moche illustrated all forms of sexual activity and combinations of participants, including masturbation, fellatio, anal intercourse, and lesbianism. And yet, as Donnan's research showed, the Moche limited their portrayals to specific activities and postures that may have had a ritualistic or ceremonial significance. Within the context of Moche art, copulation took place only between humans and supernatural creatures.

Perhaps, as Donnan suggested, the scene on the scepter depicted some kind of ultimate erotic legend, or the Moche myth of creation. But one thing was certain: The expression on the creature's face was as meaningful as the penis the creature plunged into its victim. Using giant fangs, the creature looked about to feast on the object of its desire, to kill in order to create.

However Moche scholars chose to interpret the

scepter's message, its discovery focused Donnan's attention on Huaca Rajada's importance as a potential source for more Moche artifacts, and alerted him to the excavation's desperate financial situation. Not only had Alva no film to photograph the scepter before its removal from the looted burial chamber, but excavators had no camera to put the film into.

Donnan rectified that situation by giving Alva his two Nikon cameras and more than sixty rolls of unexposed film. In an equally grand gesture, he handed Alva all the cash he had brought to Peru, approximately nine hundred dollars that he had planned to spend on excavation equipment for Pacatnamu. Donnan kept only the money he needed to return to Los Angeles.

"It's your excavation," he told his colleague, making it clear that he had no intention of using his considerable clout in the archaeological community to claim the site for himself. "I just want to see you make the most out of it."

Excited, pleased, and flushed with anticipation, Alva thanked Donnan for his generosity, then gave Montessa the long-awaited order to begin excavating the non-looted areas to see if huaqueros had overlooked anything besides the copper scepter. In giving that order, however, Alva reinforced the message that he had already sent to the villagers: that regardless of their protests, he and his excavators planned to remain at Huaca Rajada until they completed their project. Police officials understood the message as clearly as Lucho, and expressed their regret that Alva had chosen a course of action that ensured trouble.

In response, a retired police colonel, patron of the arts, and old friend of Alva's stopped off at the site to give Alva something he believed the archaeologist would need as much as Donnan's Nikon cameras and film: a box of .32-caliber shells and a black Mauser pistol.

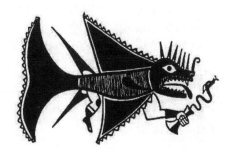

13

Over eight-thousand miles from the scorching sun and baked clay bricks of Huaca Rajada, Fred Drew's secret partner stepped out of the Holiday Inn at Marble Arch on a short trip across metropolitan London to claim the most recent shipment of smuggled Moche antiquities.

Dressed in a neatly pressed silk shirt, slacks, and blue blazer, and carrying an overcoat, the *London Times*, and a leather attaché case, thirty-year-old David Rand Swetnam bore little resemblance to the long-haired college dropout who had first traveled to Peru seven years earlier to buy tribal clothing for trendy boutiques back home in Portland, Oregon. Quick to spot a bargain, Swetnam had invested in pre-Columbian ceramics, tripled his profits, and expanded his trade route to include Bolivia, where he met his future wife, documentary-film producer Jacquelyn Sawyer. With her encouragement and his almost charismatic ability to sell art, the Swetnams relocated to Ventura County, on California's "Gold Coast," and opened Ethnos, their own pre-Columbian art gallery. Using Jacquelyn's connections in the film industry, they moved into the lavish Montecito home of Irving Azoff, then one of the highest paid executives in Hollywood, where they entertained a growing number of rich and influential clients. By the time Fred Drew came into their lives in 1984, Ethnos Gallery was well on its way to becoming the most sought after stop for pre-Columbian art in the United States.

Ernil's sudden death and the arrival of Huaca Rajada's looted treasures in London had now made it possible for Swetnam to establish an international reputation. Evidence had been forthcoming only hours earlier, when he had sold one of Drew's five-and-a-quarter-inch-long golden peanuts for twenty-two thousand dollars, a markup of more than twenty thousand dollars. Swetnam had also begun to prime the more lucrative United States market at a succession of cocktail parties and informal luncheons that he hosted at the Azoffs' Montecito mansion and at Christopher Webster's art brokerage office in Santa Fe, New Mexico. At L'Express, a stylish Los Angeles restaurant on Cahuenga Boulevard, Swetnam took advance orders from such important clients as Murray Gell-Mann, a Nobel laureate and professor of physics at Cal-Tech, the California Institute of Technology in Pasadena.

But before Swetnam could put his artifacts into the hands of his favored clients, he first had to pick them up at his private storeroom and warehouse at Fine Art Services, a short taxi ride across London, and arrange to have the antiquities put on a plane for the United States, the most dangerous leg of their journey from Peru.

A half hour after he had left his hotel room, Swetnam stood talking to Barry Cox, manager of Fine Art Services and the bonded warehouse agent Swetnam had used to pick up the Berckemeyer shipment at Heathrow Airport. Because England was not a signatory to any of the international agreements protecting the cultural heritage of countries like Peru, the only delay Cox had encountered in clearing customs was the inability of agents to decide whether to categorize the Moche artifacts as "ethnic art" or "cultural antiquities." Cox had opted for the latter.

Eager to see the artifacts, Swetnam excused himself and went into his second-floor storeroom. Nothing gave him quite the same exhilaration as seeing row upon row of precious ornaments, ancient ceramics, and statuary displayed on his shelves. And the latest arrivals, pieces that until now he had seen only in Polaroid photographs, were the best of all: large gold ear spools inlaid with semiprecious mosaics, hammered-gold figurines depicting strange and exotic deities, rattles of beaten copper, amethyst necklaces, and the golden head of a jaguar.

Delighted to see his artifacts assembled as they might have once adorned a royal Moche treasury, Swetnam hated to box them up and put them on another plane ride. But this was precisely what he did. From a corner of the narrow room, Swetnam pulled over a long metal footlocker he had purchased at Piccadilly Circus. Wooden crates might be less expensive and come in a variety of different shapes and sizes, but nothing could compare in overall strength and durability to a footlocker. Besides, the large metal door on the front could be padlocked, and its overall appearance looked more like a battered old family relic of a man's youth than an insured shipping case for pre-Columbian treasures.

Without further delay, Swetnam removed the Peruvian newspapers that Drew had used to wrap the artifacts and repackaged them in pages from that morning's edition of the London Times, which he had brought specifically for that purpose. Once he had the footlocker filled to its brim, Swetnam tossed in the crumpled raincoat, the final touch on a smuggling scheme he had first used in the summer of 1986, after customs agents in Vancouver had seized the two shipments of antiquities from Fred Drew.

The demise of the Canadian smuggling route had taught Swetnam never to have his own name associated with a shipment. For this reason, he had brought in a British partner named Michael Kelly, whose raincoat Swetnam had just packed inside the footlocker.

Swetnam had met Kelly in 1984 in Santa Barbara, when Kelly and a Pasadena antiquities dealer came to Ethnos Gallery to purchase some pre-Columbian ceramics he had recently brought from Peru. At that time, Kelly was organizing a grandiose plan for a Pan American Museum of Art in California. But after nearly five years of effort, he had managed to raise only a small portion of the financing that he needed, and his plan was no closer to fruition.

By 1986, Kelly's small Santa Barbara company, Art Collections Conservation Network, was on the verge of bankruptcy. Kelly's father, a retired film director from the Ealing film studios, had fallen seriously ill and was about to die. Swetnam agreed to pay Kelly's plane fare home to see his dying father in return for introducing him to Kelly's contacts in the British antiquities market. But the death of Kelly's father on the same day they arrived in London changed everything. Instead of introducing Swetnam to Kelly's British contacts, Kelly agreed to bring antiquities back into the United States as personal effects inherited from his father. In this way, Swetnam would not have to declare what was being imported into the United States, and at the same time, he would have a plausible "provenance" to present to his clients.

These antiquities, Swetnam and Kelly claimed, were collected in the 1920s by Michael's father, Wilfrid Kelly, a British subject born in Ceylon in 1903 who had traveled the world with explorers, scientists, and novelists, and who, through his myriad adventures, had amassed a spectacular collection of pre-Columbian objects. Michael Kelly, his sisters, and his mother had inherited this collection at Wilfrid's passing.

To complete their ruse, Swetnam had Kelly write letters that he sent to potential clients:

> I was given your name by a friend in London, he told me you would be a good person to contact with regard to various types of art, and possible sale.
>
> Presently I am with my mother sorting out the estate of my father, who recently passed away. She has asked me to sell anything which she or I do not wish to keep, so I hope you will be able to help in this matter.
>
> My father's family went to Ceylon during the latter part of the 19th c. My father was born there in 1903 and spent most of his early life exploring many parts of the world.
>
> I have been brought up surrounded by artifacts, primitive art and ancient relics, and only now have had to take responsibility for this large collection. I have been told that the U.S. is a better place to sell such things than London, so I enclose some photos to start with. If you are interested and can do something with these, then perhaps I can get the rest of the pieces photographed and send these also.
>
> The enclosed pieces are, I believe pre-Columbian and have been in my father's hands since about the 1920's. Please do not give my name or address to anyone, my mother is elderly and does not wish to be bothered by strangers.

With letters like the above already sent to clients in the United States, along with copies of Wilfrid's will and death certificate, Swetnam hadn't encountered the slightest problem moving two shipments of pre-Columbian ceramics and carvings that Drew had collected for him.

Nor had he been required to pay duty on the items, because they were considered personal effects. Even if there had been problems, Swetnam's name wasn't on the shipments.

Once he had established the smuggling route, Swetnam saw no reason not to send a third shipment, the "mother lode," as he and Jacquelyn referred to the Moche treasures from Huaca Rajada. Spreading Wilfrid Kelly's raincoat over the small packages of antiquities, then closing and padlocking the foot- locker, Swetnam knew he would have no trouble sending this shipment into the United States. The only details left to be taken care of were to have Barry Cox deliver the trunk to Pandair International Freight at Heathrow Airport and to call Michael Kelly, back in Ventura.

When Swetnam made the call to Kelly from his London hotel room, he expressed little of the real excitement that had prompted the call in the first place. He soothed any fears Kelly might have by assuring him that everything was going as planned. He told Kelly that he had stopped by his mother's home to see his family and to pick up his father's old raincoat. Almost as an aside, Swetnam said that he had obtained "one or two" additional artifacts from Fred Drew, in Peru.

"I'm sending another consignment," Swetnam told Kelly. "Just a few items that I couldn't fit into the last shipment."

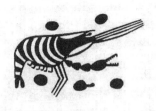

14

Until now, Alva had limited the work at the excavation site to the removal of loose brick and sand from the interior and top of the central platform and to the establishment of a base camp consisting of a pair of tents and an examination table. Once the copper scepter had been discovered and Donnan had provided the resources to excavate the non-looted areas, the base camp was enlarged to include three more tents and an outhouse to serve the needs of the eighteen new laborers Alva and Montessa hired and the six student archaeologists Alva invited to join them from the University of Trujillo. Around the base of the central platform, on the easternmost border, excavators posted signs and stretched lengths of barbed wire. High above the platform, on a knoll of excavated clay bricks overlooking the entrance to Ernil's abandoned tunnel, rose stacks of sandbags that the police used as a lookout station. The sight left a visiting journalist from the Lima Times with the impression that the archaeologists and their men looked like "soldiers," and their excavation site, an "armed camp."

With his Mauser pistol now tucked under his belt, Alva

had only himself to blame for the message sent to the villagers camped at the base of the pyramid, crowding the road leading into the site, and perched high atop the adjoining pyramid looking down at the excavators. The barbed wire around the perimeter made the notion of purely scientific, peaceful intentions impossible to sustain. But rather than ponder the practical questions that armed guards at an archaeological site raised, or seek to strengthen the lines of communication between archaeologists and town leaders, Alva focused his attention on the task at hand, concentrating on developments inside Huaca Rajada instead of those outside. And here, much as he had expected, Alva unearthed enough new archaeological evidence to warrant the risks he had taken in returning to Huaca Rajada.

Back in April, long before Alva had completed his inspection of the huaqueros' tunnels, he had assigned his now sizable labor force to begin excavating a ten-by-ten-foot opening he intended to make in the pyramid's central platform. Under Lucho's supervision, the top three layers of brick were removed from this section, lowering portions of the pyramid to the Moche underskin. In the process, Alva's men uncovered two sections of the platform near the summit where large rectangles of bricks had been cut and removed, then filled with a mixture of loosely compacted sand, soil, and small stones. In both instances, the sand, soil, and stones used to fill the rectangular cuts were clearly younger than the clay bricks surrounding them. Studying the deposits in these fills, Alva and Lucho suspected that in both cases the platform had once been opened and then resealed in Moche times.

Alva chose to explore the more accessible of the two rectangles first, an area approximately seven feet long by four feet wide, located eight feet east and two and a half feet south of the burial chamber looted by Ernil. In keeping with the architectural lines of the pyramid itself, the longest incisions had been made on a north-south axis, each apparently carefully measured before Moche craftsmen used a sharpened stone or metal blade to slice into the platform.

Following standard excavating procedures, Alva cordoned off the entire area before using teaspoons and a trowel to probe the perimeter of the rectangle. Eager as he was to uncover the entrance to a burial chamber overlooked by huaqueros, he knew from experience that the filled-in portions of the pyramid could well be a design flaw in its construction, or a chamber that Moche builders may no longer have had a purpose for and sealed up, much like renovations made on an old house by its latest tenants. At Pacatnamu, dozens of such rooms had been discovered, the majority containing little more than compacted soil or crushed brick. But regardless of whether the incisions marked the entrance to an abandoned room or merely a design flaw, their presence intrigued Alva and his men.

Indeed, Alva and his men had every right to be intrigued, for late in the afternoon of June 14, once excavators had painstakingly removed the first two and a half feet of soil and sand from inside the rectangle, the imprint of a wooden beam, long since rotted away, could be clearly seen crisscrossing the rectangular space they had cleared under the incisions. Further cleaning revealed at least seven more wooden beams, three of which were more than ten feet long and seven inches wide. All seven had carefully been cut and fitted into supporting grooves or postholes that had been carved into the sides of the wall to accommodate them.

Although Alva had never encountered a construction technique quite like this, the purpose of the beams and their arrangement across the rectangle of packed earth clearly indicated that they had once functioned as the roof for some kind of chamber beneath them. But thousands or more years of sand sifting through the roof had gradually filled the chamber, covering its contents in a thick blanket. Tablespoons, dustpans, and paintbrushes in hand, Alva and Lucho began the laborious and time-consuming process of peeling back the blanket.

Once the flick of a brush bared the lid of a red clay pot, tedium vanished. Now every brush stroke exposed another small pot, then a bowl, a beaker, a jar or vase. As the hours passed, archaeologists inventoried more than three hundred ceramics, all clearly of Moche design and many clustered in unusual formations around piles of llama bones and corroded pieces of copper. By the end of the next evening, after Alva and his men had removed the entire top layer of silt from the four-and-a-half-foot-deep chamber, more than fifteen hundred individual pots had been counted, the largest and most spectacular cache of Moche ceramics ever to be excavated.

As archaeologists had long known, the Moche created ceramics for a myriad of religious or ceremonial uses. Donnan, in *Moche Art of Peru,* had gone on at great length to demonstrate just how deceptive those uses might be. A bottle that appeared to present a deer hunt for food might actually portray a ritual in which Moche lords, seated on a litter, ceremonially killed a deer. Depictions of sea lion hunts actually portrayed the ritual quest for stones in the sea lion's stomach that the Moche believed possessed magical properties.

Moche ceramics like those Alva had studied as a youth often bore intricate iconography in red and beige patterns. Kaleidoscopic at first sight, these patterns resolved themselves upon closer inspection into "themes" of ritual, sacrifice, combat, and ceremony. Another sizable portion of Moche ceramics depicted warriors, hunchbacks, women giving birth, agonized prisoners pinned to racks, and erotic sexual encounters. Even more plentiful were depictions of animals, plants, and insects. Among the most popular scenes appeared to be ghost-white skeletonized death figures holding hands and dancing in a funeral procession to the accompaniment of musicians playing panpipes.

The precise reason why quantities of these ceramics accompanied Moche burials always remained a mystery, but researchers assumed that the ceramics were placed in the graves for the dead to take into the Moche netherworld, and that the quantity and type of ceramic object directly related to the stature and social role of the interred. Iconographic depictions of burial ceremonies portraying stacks of ceramic vessels overflowing with food and other libations tended to support this notion. At Huaca Rajada, Alva and his men now had an unparalleled opportunity to test those assumptions.

Like elves, a thousand or more clay beakers sculpted to portray miniature people crowded together in the hollowed-out rectangle. Their coarse surfaces, the absence of wear, and their often identical shapes betrayed them as copies of a few basic designs, mass-produced in molds. Mold-made pottery, however, didn't lessen its value to the Moche or its importance to archaeologists. Quite the contrary. Even the much sought after portrait-head bottles and stirrup-spouts were made in two-piece molds. The early introduction of molds and stamps brought efficiency to the Moche production process, making it available to a wide range of people, and also permitting archaeologists to quantify innovations and development more easily. Alva could put a fairly accurate date on a particular Moche grave merely by examining the ceramics that accompanied it.

Without question, Alva and Lucho had discovered more Moche ceramics in one place than archaeologists had ever unearthed. To add to their excitement, a second cache of pottery was discovered in a nearby chamber containing two or three hundred more ceramics clustered into specific scenes or arrangements. Because of their sheer number, Alva and Lucho agreed that the pieces had enormous religious or ceremonial significance. Because of their similarity, or continuity of theme, Alva and Lucho also knew that they had been created specifically for the purpose of interment in the chamber where excavators had discovered them. Judging by their style and design, they had been placed in the chamber around the year A.D. 200, a period of great expansion for the Moche.

In the arrangements or scenes Alva unearthed in the second ceramic chamber, prisoners sat naked and suffered the humiliation of leash-like rope collars. Musicians clutched drums and panpipes. High officials or members of a court looked haughtily at the prisoners behind tight-lipped smiles, their throats hung with necklaces and their earlobes adorned with large ornaments. More important officials, perhaps regional rulers or clan leaders, puffed their chests beneath beaded pectorals, or kissed the air in salutation of a lord or god. Few of the ceramic figures had arms or legs. As Alva later explained to his student excavators, "Ceramic sculptures that had no legs could not climb out of the sacrificial chamber."

A cursory examination revealed clues to the order or nature of the ceramic arrangements. Musicians and prisoners, for example, ringed and faced nobler personages or trooped past in double file. A few figures, perhaps high priests, posed alone and apart, contemplating a half-shell of spondylus, a type of oyster venerated in Andean tradition as food for the gods. Other figures meditated before deposits of llama bones, an animal prized throughout Peruvian history because it yielded wool for garments and dung for fertilizer and fires, while serving as a long-distance freight carrier.

Alva and Lucho could only speculate, but it seemed clear to them that the entire contents of the ceramic chambers illustrated an enormous funeral ceremony in miniature. If so, the burial that brought the procession together must have been of the highest rank, for a macabre final discovery awaited the archaeologists in a small niche cut into the bottom of the ceramic chamber.

In a space that measured approximately three and a half feet high by four feet wide were the human remains of what appeared to have been a young man. Looking as if he had been a contortionist, the man's skeleton lay jackknifed on his back, with chin, crossed arms, and knees all forced into a joint-popping tuck. Viewed from above, he resembled a bony embryo, or, more precisely, a corpse bent in half. Unfortunately, his remains were so badly decomposed, and his bones so fragmented as a result of his burial position, that next to nothing could be told about how he had come to assume such a position, only that he had undoubtedly been dead before being squeezed into the small opening in the chamber floor.

Another section of the chamber contained several semicircular copper sheets, once part of elaborate headdresses, and a naturalistic human mask, also made of copper, resting beside a pile of llama bones. Because of the placement of these objects at the opposite end of the chamber, neither the bones nor the ornaments appeared to be the personal property of the contortionist: evidence that his status could not have been so exalted as to require llama sacrifices or the hasty manufacture of a huge collection of ceramics.

Perhaps, as Alva suggested to Lucho, he could have been a sacrificial offering or voluntary suicide buried to honor someone of much higher rank entombed in another crypt or hidden chamber. As Lucho poured acrylic over the bones and lifted the contortionist out of the niche he had been buried in, Alva and Lucho had the same idea: The answer could be found in the rectangular cut adjacent to the one they had just excavated.

15

Excavation into the second cut began at sunrise on June 15 and continued uninterrupted until ten-thirty A.M. on June 18, the morning Montessa's spade exposed the rotted fragments of cotton cloth covering a human bone. "A burial ... a burial. . ." he shouted, unable to contain his excitement.

Moments later, Lucho joined Montessa at the bottom of the rectangular pit that he and his men had cleared of compacted soil. Montessa's judgment, though premature, turned out to be correct. At a depth of twelve feet beneath the platform floor, his spade had unearthed traces of a cotton bundle containing cane, bone, and corroded copper: the telltale signs of a Moche burial.

Further examination could not take place until laborers constructed scaffolding that would allow archaeologists to probe the cotton bundle without putting unnecessary weight on the surrounding area, perhaps crushing bones or artifacts underneath. Building the raised platform, plus the tedious process of brushing aside the loose earth, kept the actual contents of the bundle a secret from excavators until the end of the month, prompting Montessa, a former huaquero, to remark that he "could have been inside the tomb in ten minutes."

In the twelve hours it took excavators to clean and expose the burial, almost everyone in camp speculated about the possibilities. In view of the quantity of the ceramic offerings in the adjoining chamber and the splendor of the gold and silver artifacts that the police had seized in the raid on the Bernal house, expectations had never been higher that a significant Moche burial had been located.

As more of the compacted soil was brushed away, there appeared the remains of a human skeleton stretched out on its back, arms at its sides, head to the east, feet to the west. A forensic examination performed later by Dr. John Verano, a physical anthropologist brought to Huaca Rajada by Chris Donnan, confirmed Alva's initial hypothesis that the skeleton was an adult male, approximately twenty years old, and apparently in good health at the time of his death. Lumps of copper about the size of silver dollars still lay where they had been slipped into the dead man's left hand and mouth, a common upper- class Moche ritual that suggested that some form of payment was needed before an individual could pass into the Moche netherworld, a custom similar to the ancient Greek practice of putting coins into the hands of their dead for passage across the River Styx.

In terms of antiquities or treasures, the burial yielded surprisingly little. Two of the most significant possessions that accompanied the bones were a cone-shaped gilded-copper helmet placed on the skeleton's head and a circular gilded-copper shield placed across his chest. Extensive corrosion on both made it impossible to see any iconographic detail that may have once existed on them. In addition, centuries of pressure from the tons of compacted soil that filled the top of the chamber had so flattened and misshapen the artifacts that they were almost impossible to separate from the remains of the skeleton's head and chest bones. In spite of the deterioration, however, these possessions provided clear evidence to Alva that the skeleton belonged to a Moche warrior or high military official, not royalty, as archaeologists had hoped.

Distinctive cone-shaped helmets decorated with large plumes of feathers, bangles, or carved ornaments were commonly pictured on Moche ceramics, as were round shields decorated with symbols or designs that suggested membership in a particular clan. Identical helmets and shields had also been excavated from the graves of Moche warriors at numerous archaeological sites, the mouths or hands of many of the warriors often containing similar lumps of copper. In some high-ranking burials, weapons had been found tied together into bundles.

Moche art frequently depicted military equipment, warriors, and activities that warriors were involved in. Quite often, ceramics showed warriors parading in front of royalty, as if in preparation for war. Other scenes were of warriors using clubs to beat the heads of enemies or hurling stones and arrows by means of a sling. Like scenes portraying sexual acts and sacrifice, however, depictions of warriors in combat or engaged in other activities were limited in scope and appeared to follow a consistent set of rules.

As Donnan first pointed out, Moche warriors were never shown in the process of overthrowing an opposing army. Rather, warriors, like gladiators in a Roman amphitheater, participated in hand-to-hand combat on an open field or raised platform or in an arena. Participants fought in pairs or groups, but always one-on-one and with similar types of weapons. Their ultimate goal, unlike their Roman counterparts, appeared to be the capture of prisoners for torture and presentation at the sacrifice ceremony.

A complex set of rules may have governed the conduct

of Moche warriors off and on the field, from their face paint, clothing, and the ornaments displayed on their uniforms to the types of weapons that could be used during combat. Battles ended when one warrior caught hold of another's hair, a sign of supplication in ancient Andean culture. Once he was captured, the clothes and weapons of the prisoner were removed and hung in bundles from the war club of his captor, and the prisoner was then paraded past Moche royalty before being sacrificed. Depending upon his luck or skill, a Moche warrior was either prey or predator, paying for his defeat in the coin of his own capture, loss of respect, and eventual dismemberment.

Like Maya royalty, Moche lords or noblemen may have gone into battle themselves, for many scenes portrayed a defeated ruler or lord stripped of his finery and presented to his rival for torture and sacrifice. Face paint, clothing, and other iconographic details also suggested that lords and their warriors battled only other Moche lords and warriors, not invaders from another culture, as previous generations of Andean scholars had believed. Moche lords may not have even maintained a standing army, but relied solely on the combat prowess of themselves and their warriors to capture prisoners.

Barbarous and sadistic as the Moche's practice may seem by contemporary standards, their capacity to conduct "mock" battles may have played an important developmental role in their society, just as athletic contests held in "ball-courts" served their contemporaries, the Maya. Alva had given this subject much thought earlier in his career, but had been unable draw any definitive conclusions because archaeologists had never found any physical evidence that Moche warriors actually competed for prisoners or that a sacrifice ceremony had been conducted. All Alva could be sure about was a warrior's high social status as a member of the privileged class in

Moche society. Various types and ranks of warriors must have existed within the class as a whole and were presumably differentiated by the shape and design of headdresses and weaponry, face paint, tattoos, and special skills.

Based on iconographic evidence, Alva assumed that the warrior Montessa had unearthed could well be deserving of an important pyramid burial. He could have honored a lord in combat, or presented a particularly high-ranking sacrifice for ritual torture at the sacrifice ceremony. Just as true, however, was the possibility that he could have been a sacrifice himself.

Had depictions of warriors on Moche art and iconography been all he had to base his judgment on, Alva would have ordered the skeleton exhumed and then moved on to a more promising section of the pyramid. In the case of this warrior, however, other clues led Alva to take a second, closer look at the grave and its contents.

A puzzling aspect of this burial was the absence of a war club, sheath of darts, combat mace, scepter, or any other paraphernalia commonly associated with the warrior class. Except for the helmet and shield, the grave contained nothing at all to warrant the cache of ceramics and sacrifices associated with it. Nor was the warrior buried with his head to the south and his feet to the north, a practice common to every Moche burial Alva had excavated. And as Alva had learned from Max Diaz, the Moche left nothing to chance. A cursory look at how the skeleton of the warrior's hand was curled around the lump of copper, the care taken to straighten out its arms and legs, and the position of his shield told Alva that every detail about this burial had been planned.

Besides the helmet and shield, Alva discovered a ten-inch sharpened bone or spear head beneath the body. Because of the placement of the bone directly under the skeleton's back, the sharpened instrument appeared less a treasured possession than a potential clue to his death. Deterioration of the skeletal remains, however, made it impossible to tell how the warrior had lost his life. Decomposition of the cotton wrapping beside it also made it impossible to ascertain if a wooden shaft had once been attached to the sharpened bone. Yet the man's fate was certainly out of the ordinary because Alva found no trace of the skeleton's feet. Either these had somehow deteriorated at a faster rate than the rest of the skeletal remains, or they had been amputated.

Alva suspected amputation. Just as the jackknifed man may have given his life as a sacrifice, so too had the warrior. For the same reasons that so few of the pots in the ceramic cache had legs, this warrior's feet had been amputated to assure his continued presence at the site, his responsibility to remain forever at his post, vigilant and on guard.

But guarding whom or what?

Alva asked himself this question as Lucho carefully painted acrylic preservative over the warrior's bones and hoisted them out of the chamber as if quarrying a stone. Alva's only logical answer was that this warrior had been sacrificed as a kind of "guardian" to protect a Moche lord buried in a chamber Alva and his men had yet to unearth.

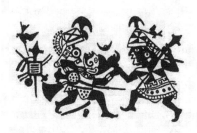

16

Excavating on two or three hours of sleep, Alva and Lucho completed their examination of the fifteen-square-foot stratum of adobe bricks around the final corner of the opening in the platform. Then, certain that no hidden niches had been overlooked, they began removing one spoonful of clay fill at a time, lowering the chamber floor inch by inch until the top of Alva's wide-brimmed straw hat disappeared beneath the bricks at the top of the platform, and Montessa and his men had to stand directly above the opening to see the progress being made inside.

Further evidence of the special nature of this chamber came to light in the flat, rectangular faces of a dozen or more bricks set into the walls. Here, Moche craftsmen had used sharpened blades to carve tridents, circles, crosses, and curling waves. Each marking, about six inches high and four inches wide, had been positioned in one of the four cardinal points of the compass, perhaps symbolizing the four forces of the Moche universe: air, earth, sea, and heaven. Another possibility was that the markings represented ancient pictographs, or hieroglyphs. If so, Alva and Lucho had uncovered startling new evidence that the Moche possessed the rudiments of a basic writing system, an advancement far beyond the repertoire of skills that most archaeologists accorded them.

Lack of a writing system among the otherwise advanced cultures of Peru had long puzzled scholars and historians. The Aztecs, prior to the arrival of the conquistadors, had a form of pictographic writing that had reached the stage of syllabic phonetics. The Maya were as far advanced as the Egyptians, as evidenced by the permanent record of their history and achievements that they left behind in glyphs on stone and on paper. Even the North American Plains Indian tribes had a form of rebus pictograph writing through which they were able to convey ideas.

But the closest that the ancient cultures of Peru, Ecuador, and Brazil apparently came to a writing system was an Inca device known as a *quipu*, which consisted of a string of intertwining colored threads and knots that was relayed by messengers running from outpost to outpost, covering hundreds, perhaps thousands, of miles. A particular class of Inca royalty, trained to read the colored patterns and knots, was charged with interpreting the messages. Unfortunately, no archaeologists ever found a quipu and all modern scholars had to base their studies on were early accounts of Inca life by missionaries and conquistadors.

Rafael Larco Hoyle, one of the pioneers of pre-Inca scholarship, advanced the theory that the Moche possessed a form of hieroglyphic language that they inscribed on lima beans and transmitted through a system of runners, from whom the Inca later derived their own system. According to this system, advanced by Larco in a report published in Buenos Aires in 1944, a particular type of lima bean, known as a *pallares*, was incised with various dots and symbols, then taken from one location to another in leather pouches carried by messengers.

Larco based his theory on both iconographic depictions and archaeological evidence. His iconographic depictions consisted of scenes familiar to almost every student of Moche art: runners wearing highly specialized headgear carrying pouches across the desert, and groups of royalty or priests examining the lima beans. For archaeological evidence, Larco claimed to have excavated a Moche grave containing a leather pouch made from a well-tanned, soft piece of llama hide. Inside were painted pallares.

As Larco illustrated in his paper, analogies could be drawn between the Maya glyphs and those of the Moche. His comparisons, ingenious by any standards, raised both interest and criticism from Moche and Maya scholars alike. In one example, a Moche fox was pictured handling what are obviously pallares painted with different symbols, which Larco compared to a Maya figure of a fox with glyphs painted above it. A second example consisted of a Moche figure of an anthropomorphized bird painting symbols on lima beans and a Maya figure engaged in the same activity.

As provocative as this theory was, Larco died before he published his supporting evidence, and a later generation of archaeologists advanced the theory that the painted lima beans and bean-bag runners represented some form of ancient gambling or game playing, not a primitive communications system. Although archaeologists of Donnan's stature scoffed at Larco's theory for being unscientific, Alva had always been interested in exploring it further.

But discovery of the strange markings in the bricks at Huaca Rajada neither supported nor disputed Larco's theory, for Alva and Lucho could find no hard evidence to classify the markings as anything other than decorative symbols, and none of the Huaca Rajada markings appeared to match those on Larco's lima beans. All Alva and Lucho could say for certain was that this strange chamber, regardless of its purpose or use, had been laid open for a period of time, perhaps months, before its contents were placed inside.

Twenty inches beneath the markings, Alva and Lucho again found the telltale traces of wooden beams. Though the beams themselves had long ago disintegrated, the posthole indentations they left in the clay bricks lining the chamber and a few crumbly fragments of the decomposed wood told Alva all he needed to know about them. Probably cut from algaroba trees, as many as seventeen rough-hewn timbers, eight inches in diameter and thirteen feet long, had been laid along an east-west axis, resting on a pair of cross supports to form a ceiling on an inner sub-chamber carved into the pyramid beneath them. Radiocarbon tests obtained later gave a date for this assembly as A.D. 290, plus or minus half a century, about the same time that craftsmen installed the cache of ceramics previously excavated, and the same time period in which the Moche were believed to have reached the apogee of economic and creative dominion over the north coast.

By now, Alva was able to interpret the discovery of wood as a harbinger of discoveries to come. However, the layout and configuration of the decomposed wood differed significantly from that of the beams covering the two ceramic caches. Layers of sediment and the gray discoloration of decomposing wood revealed that the timbering had slumped a foot or more, indicating a caved-in roof and hollowed-out inner chamber beneath. As the wooden beams had begun to rot, the great weight of the mountain of earth filling the chamber above had caused the beams to bend and separate. This pressure had then forced a fine silt to sprinkle into the chamber beneath, eventually covering its contents like the blanket of sediment that had covered the ceramics cache.

No one else in Peruvian archaeology had ever reported

discovering such an inner chamber. Not even Hiram Bingham, the American archaeologist who had first hiked the mountainous slopes to Machu Picchu, or Julio Tello, the man who had contributed more to an understanding of his nation's archaeological past than anyone else. And yet, Alva thought not of them but of Max Diaz, who was haunting Alva's every move, cautioning him to take his time and not risk inflicting harm on what might lie beneath the rotted timbers. "Patience," Diaz always said, "not technical virtuosity or skill, separated the professional from the amateur."

Alva was reminded of the story about Howard Carter, the British Egyptologist renowned for his slow and painstaking archaeological technique. After finding the sealed doorway leading into Tutankhamun's tomb, on the verge of what might be a unique discovery in the history of Egyptian archaeology, a moment when his associates were in the highest state of excitement imaginable, Carter knelt on his hands and knees to examine potsherds and other ancient debris that had been used to fill the approach to the tomb entrance. Carter's meticulous examination paid off because the debris contained evidence that this precious tomb had been opened and then resealed in ancient times. A single potsherd, inscribed with the name of Tutankhamun, found in the ton or more of debris hauled out of the passage, held a secret that explained the disordered contents of the tomb they were about to excavate.

Following Carter's example and Max Diaz's maxim, Lucho and Alva spent the next three days sketching and photographing the various levels of the chamber and sunken roof before carefully removing centuries of powdery silt from the upper portion of the inner chamber. By June 15, at nine-thirty A.M., enough silt had been brushed away to reveal a sight that left Alva and Lucho transfixed: a peacock-green sheaf of copper ribbon, so artfully crafted that the corroded metal resembled leather lashings. Nearby was another green sheaf of metal, and a third and fourth, each composed of the same corroded green copper. Three days later, Alva and Lucho had dusted off another four enigmatic metal straps. Together, they marked the four corners and sides of a rectangular area four feet wide and seven feet long, faintly imprinted by three vanished wooden planks.

Unable to imagine the purpose of the straps, or the planking, Alva awaited the impending arrival of Christopher Donnan, who was paying a second visit to the site on his way to reopen his annual summer excavation at Pacatnamu. Donnan parked his Chevy truck at the base of the pyramid on the afternoon of June 20, pushed through a small crowd of curious villagers on the path to the top of the platform, and stood beside Alva and Lucho on the scaffolding above the exposed chamber.

Donnan had a good idea of what the copper straps might be. But it wasn't the two caches of ceramics, the presence of the guardian, or the strange, carved markings that tipped him off. During the two months that had elapsed since the discovery of the copper scepter, Donnan had examined and photographed more than a hundred gold and silver ornaments, beaded bracelets, golden ear spools, and other artifacts of clothing and ceremony plundered from Huaca Rajada.

Like Alva, Donnan had come to the conclusion that Ernil and his men had indeed plundered the tomb of a Moche lord. But Donnan had taken Alva's analysis one step further by making a more precise identification of the looted burial possessions. Although the artifacts shared many similar artistic themes, variations in the amount of detail and embellishment suggested that they had come from the tombs of at least two Moche lords, and that three hundred or more years had elapsed between their burials.

Unless Donnan was mistaken, a "likely possibility," he freely admitted, the chamber that Alva was now excavating contained the remains of yet another Moche lord.

Looking down at the enigmatic straps, Donnan told Lucho and Alva just what he guessed they were, but kept his voice lowered to prevent his message from being carried to the villagers gathered outside the perimeter of the looted platform. "It's the royal coffin," Donnan said. "Never opened."

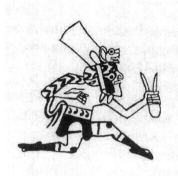

17

As Alva and Lucho peered anxiously into one royal Moche burial chamber, the partial contents from two others arrived in Los Angeles from London on Pan American cargo flight 125. Prepared to claim the shipment, fine-art consultant and restoration specialist Michael Kelly sat in the passenger seat of his partner's blue Toyota pickup truck, completely unaware that the one-million-dollar cargo consigned to him could send him to prison on charges ranging from fraud to trafficking in stolen art.

Prior to being notified of the shipment, Kelly had received two earlier consignments, one on November 4 of the year before, and another in May 1987. The contents had been the same: ten to fourteen Inca and pre-Inca ceramics and textiles worth a few thousand dollars, unlikely to attract the attention of customs authorities. Each time, David Swetnam had packed the footlocker in London and forwarded it to him in Los Angeles. Kelly had claimed the artifacts at Pan Am's bonded warehouse, paid the freight out of his own business account, then delivered them to the Azoff mansion in Montecito. In return, Kelly had received twenty-five hundred dollars in cash, the round-trip plane fare to London, and four Brazilian gold coins.

Now, for reasons that were still not clear to Kelly, David Swetnam had changed their routine. Swetnam had been edgy and preoccupied since his last trip to Peru and his return from England. Instead of sending Kelly to pick up the third shipment alone, Swetnam had called to say that he would be accompanying him from Santa Barbara to LAX. At first, Kelly was pleased to have Swetnam join him. He appreciated having company on the two-and-a-half-hour trip. He also mistakenly believed that the more favors he did for his partner, the sooner Swetnam and his clients would help him to realize his dream of opening a pre-Columbian art museum in Los Angeles.

But Swetnam was not interested in talking about Kelly's plans to open a museum. As they pulled off the San Diego freeway into the maze of access roads leading to the offices of Pandair International Freight, all Swetnam wanted to talk about was the shipment from London and what would happen when they reached the airport. While Swetnam waited in the car, Kelly would pay the freight charges and collect the bill of lading at Pandair. Swetnam would then drive Kelly to the Pan Am bonded warehouse to pick up the footlocker, and they would soon be back on the freeway, this time heading to Santa Monica to visit one of Swetnam's customers. In return for signing his name to the shipment, Kelly would pocket a quick twenty-five hundred dollars. "Nothing could be easier," Swetnam told Kelly in the parking lot.

Everything went as Swetnam had said it would. Kelly wrote a check for thirty dollars drawn on his Santa Barbara business account—Art Collections Conservation Network—and obtained airbill #56271754. A few minutes later, he picked up the footlocker at Pan Am's bonded warehouse and declared its contents "personal effects." No duty had to be paid on the cargo because the shipment fell under the duty-free provisions of the Tariff Act. Customs agents passed the shipment through without looking inside.

Kelly's surprise came after Swetnam helped him to load the footlocker into the back of the truck and drove out of the parking lot. Mimicking a triumphant running back who has scored a touchdown, Swetnam raised his fist into the air and yelled at the top of his lungs. But Kelly still didn't understand what the celebration was about until after they exited the freeway and pulled up beside a green Jaguar sedan parked in front of 210 Twenty-second Street, a modest two-story Spanish-style house in a quiet residential area of Santa Monica. At Swetnam's request, Kelly helped to lug the 116-pound footlocker into the living room, where Swetnam showed its contents to Ben Johnson, one of the ten clients to whom Swetnam had chosen to reveal his "little secret."

At age forty-nine, Benjamin Bishop Johnson was a highly respected art specialist and pre-Columbian expert, having single-handedly organized the Los Angeles County Museum of Art's conservation department and acted as an adviser to such prominent collectors as Norton Simon, Armand Hammer, and Edward Carter. Before coming to Los Angeles in 1967, Johnson had begun his professional career in Washington, D.C., as conservator of American paintings at the Freer Gallery of Art and as a restoration specialist at Dumbarton Oaks, the National Portrait Gallery, and the Smithsonian Institution. But Johnson's brilliant mind was trapped in an ailing body. Juvenile diabetes had led to four kidney transplants, amputation of both legs, a heart bypass, and a weekly hookup to a dialysis machine. As a consequence, he had retired to private practice since 1979: collecting, authenticating, and selling art to the richest and most influential clients in

America.

Kelly had met Johnson on a dozen or more occasions before this. He had also written Johnson one of the letters that he and Swetnam had concocted back in London, should Kelly ever have trouble at customs or Johnson need a "provenance" for one of the artifacts from Peru. But in spite of their previous meetings and the letter on file in Johnson's office, Kelly still didn't appreciate the true value or significance of the shipment he had just picked up from LAX. Not until Swetnam cleared a place on the living-room floor beside Johnson's grand piano, produced the key to the footlocker, flung it open, and tossed aside his father's old overcoat did the truth finally sink in.

Underneath the coat were thirty to forty small boxes and an equal number of ceramics and assorted other items. Swetnam and Johnson started to giggle as Swetnam tossed his client one of the boxes and asked him to open it. Giggles turned to laughter as Johnson unwrapped one shining gold bead after another from a massive necklace and placed them on the dining-room table. As thin and emaciated as Johnson's last operation had left him, his face began to flush bright red as he spoke the names of prestigious collectors and institutions awaiting the artifacts. It seemed to Kelly that everyone in the pre-Columbian field had been in on Swetnam's smuggling scheme except himself.

Before they finished unpacking the footlocker, Swetnam and Johnson had covered the dining-room table with large golden ear spools inlaid with semiprecious mosaics, necklaces of gold and amethyst, and figurines of warriors, pumas, and mysterious deities made of beaten copper covered with gold. Kelly had a hard time believing his eyes. To clients like Johnson and a dozen others on Swetnam's Rolodex, the artifacts in front of him were worth a hundred times the value of the two previous shipments.

Johnson confirmed exactly what Kelly had only been thinking. In all the years he had been in business, Johnson had never seen a shipment of pre-Columbian objects as rich in beauty and history as those before him. Here was the real thing. Not even major suppliers like Ken Klausson in Colombia, or buyers like Jonathan Hill in San Francisco and Alan Sawyer in Canada, could get their hands on such masterpieces. Just to look at his own reflection in one of the sculpted gold tumi knives took Johnson's breath away. Literally. After ten minutes of holding the items that Swetnam pulled out of the footlocker, Johnson had to be wheeled into his book-lined bedroom to rest.

Kelly also needed to rest. But not from looking at the cardboard boxes and the treasures inside them. For twenty-five hundred dollars he had risked smuggling artifacts worth in excess of one million dollars into the United States. His partner had used him, taken him for a fool.

And he had been a fool. Angered, outraged, Kelly would decide to strike back, to steal from the master thief himself. Besides, he considered a portion of the pieces to be rightfully his. He had signed for them, and he had taken all the risk.

Before Swetnam returned from helping Johnson out of his wheelchair and into bed, Kelly reached into the footlocker and took a box containing two chains of gold and orchid-colored beads that Ernil had plucked out of the tomb at Huaca Rajada six months before. During those six months, Pereda had cleaned and polished the beads, Fred Drew had strung them together, Miguel Berckemeyer had put them on a plane for England, and Michael Kelly had smuggled them into the United States. Ernil and his brothers had been paid the equivalent of thirty dollars for the beads. Fred Drew had purchased them from Ernesto for sixty-five dollars. Now David Swetnam intended to sell them to Ben Johnson for fifteen hundred dollars.

PART 4

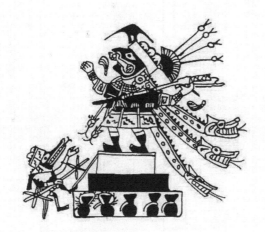

LORD OF SIPAN

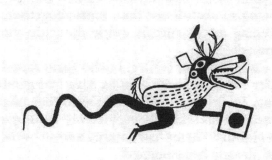

18

Huaqueros had begun to spread rumors about the existence of a second un-looted burial chamber inside Huaca Rajada even before Lucho poured preservative over the bones of the guardian and hoisted his remains into the museum van. By July 1, 1987, however, as excavators cleared the loose earth from the copper straps that had once secured the planks of a coffin, teams of huaqueros who had previously been content to shout obscenities and threats at "Ernil's murderers" now massed behind the barbed wire to hurl rocks and shout for their "ancestors' inheritance."

Alberto Jaime, the most outspoken protester, brandished a small-caliber pistol that police investigators suspected had been given to him by Poli and the Bernal brothers. At night, as police fired rounds of shots over his head in a futile attempt to frighten him, Jaime and Eulogio Galvez, a man known to criminal authorities as "Pipa" because of his height, fired shots back, encouraging the crowds to "take justice into their own hands."

Huaca Rajada's two patrolmen, assigned to the site by Assistant Police Chief Temoche, responded by increasing the number of patrols and restricting the traffic of cars and people coming to and going from the site. No one except the police ventured beyond the compound after sunset. Laborers and student archaeologists abandoned their tents altogether, choosing to make sleeping arrangements inside the excavation pits or huaqueros' tunnels.

Less at ease than ever before, Lucho again raised the issue of his transfer to another site. But as Alva had gambled from the beginning, Lucho's curiosity about what they might find in the tomb overcame his fear of being attacked by huaqueros. After all, not even Howard Carter had entered a royal burial chamber that had not already been opened.

Alva had turned his back on the hostilities and retreated into the excavation pit he now considered home. Like Lucho, he slept in the burial chamber, a few feet away from the royal coffin, one hand on a tarp that they had stretched across the top of the coffin to protect it from glass bottles or rocks thrown from above. In Alva's other hand, he kept the black Mauser pistol, loaded and ready to fire.

"Help will come," Alva insisted each morning as he tried to raise the fading morale of his men. But since Alva never elaborated on the specifics, his words did little to dispel the fears that each excavator gradually came to accept as truth: that Temoche and Mondragon had no more reinforcements to send to Huaca Rajada and that the number of huaqueros coming to the site was increasing with each passing hour.

Had Alva's enthusiasm not been so contagious, or evidence of the tomb's lavish contents not been forthcoming, Montessa, his men, and the student archaeologists might have abandoned the site before huaqueros had them completely surrounded. But Montessa and his men remained, first clearing the brick from around the sides of the chamber, then looking over Alva's and

Lucho's shoulders as the two archaeologists bent over the imprints of the coffin's wooden planks as carefully as surgeons laboring over life.

A familiar shape started to take form. Like an Egyptian mummy within its sarcophagus, its proportions were all too human: about six feet long and two feet wide. Unlike its Egyptian counterpart, however, this mummy had no clear lines as delineated by multiple wrappings, but looked something like a flattened bean pod or squashed cocoon. Quickly, Alva and Lucho understood that the artifacts and bones in the coffin were layered and somewhat jumbled, disturbed by the gradual decomposition of the body inside and the fall of the chamber roof.

Dust and sediment gave way under Alva's tweezers to a mantle composed of fragments of gilded copper platelets, much like those Ricardo Zapata had looted from the site before coming to work for Alva. Alongside these platelets were carved turquoise beads backed with tobacco-brown fabric. Carefully stitched together with cotton thread, the mantle consisted of two separate weavings about two feet long and two feet wide. The first weaving was embellished with four small copper figures of a single man with a crescent-shaped nose ring, circular ear spools, and turquoise bracelets, all in raised relief. The other bore a larger representation of the same man, also with bracelets and nose ring. In broad-legged stance, with arms upraised and fists clenched, he brought to mind a cartoon of a circus strongman flexing his biceps. Unless Alva had misunderstood its significance, the emblem on this mantle could be the personal emblem or insignia for Moche lords.

A V-shaped headdress of gilded copper sheeting two feet across, discovered just beneath the weavings, bore yet another figure of the man with the same nose ring, ear spools, and turquoise bracelets. This time, however, the figure thrust out his chest in raised relief, wearing a necklace composed of individual beads depicting the heads of giant owls. The V formed by his outstretched hands flared widely, his palms open as if in an attitude of divine sacrament.

Lifting a small clod of sediment beside a copper sheet, Alva exchanged glances with a pair of tiny gold-and-turquoise eyes. Leaning in to take a closer look, Alva could see that they belonged to a meticulously detailed miniature man made of hammered sheet gold, clad in a turquoise tunic and crowned by a massive, moon-shaped headdress.

No larger than Alva's thumb, this sprite was without doubt the finest, most valuable single item of jewelry from pre-Columbian America that had ever been excavated, for only under a microscope could the exacting craftsmanship of its creators be truly appreciated. Ironically, at least one similar artifact had been unearthed in one of the looted tombs, but huaqueros had thoughtlessly shorn the artifact from its backing and, in their haste, misplaced or lost the myriad miniature accoutrements that made the figurine so unique a work of art.

A tiny war club, seemingly gripped in his right hand, slid free to the touch. A gold ornament in the shape of a half-moon swung from the septum of his nose, just as it might in real life. A removable miniature necklace consisted of eight gold owl's heads, each strung with gold wire through microscopic perforations. Tiny crescent-shaped rattles, exactly like the one seized in the raid on the Bernal house, swung from the little man's belt. Tendons in his gold legs stretched taut, the muscles on his arms bulged.

Equally impressive were the carved turquoise figures of two attendants standing next to the little man in a circle of gold. Each was about the size of a thumb nail, and each held a circular disk. Only after reassembling scattered bits of gold and turquoise that surrounded this homunculus did

Alva discover the little man to be the three-dimensional centerpiece of a large ear ornament.

As spectacular and beautiful as this object was to look at, iconographic depictions on Moche ceramics taught Alva that this was not art for art's sake, but the representation of a Moche lord accompanied by two priests of the royal Moche court. Here, in front of him, in golden ornaments so small that Alva could fit them all into the palm of his hand, was a miniature inventory of the treasures of the tomb that lay beneath their fingertips.

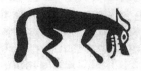

19

Lucho pleaded with Alva to carve trenches around the remains of the coffin, slide planks beneath it, and hoist the contents of the tomb out of the burial chamber. Either this, Lucho said, or Alva had better practice firing his pistol, because two patrolmen in the lookout station couldn't begin to hold back the teeming mob of two hundred huaqueros and villagers estimated to be massed just outside the perimeter of the platform.

Alva listened to Lucho's impassioned appeal to move the burial to the museum, but remained as committed to a full excavation as he had been from the beginning, once again invoking Max Diaz's cardinal rule of archaeology: not to rush an excavation. Doing so meant overlooking the smaller, seemingly unimportant details—the "tiny brush strokes," as Diaz called them—that in the long run proved to be the clues to the mystery of how the artifacts were placed in the tomb. To cut trenches around the remains jeopardized any artifacts or burials elsewhere in the tomb. Transporting the artifacts along the un- paved roads back to the museum would certainly shift the positions of artifacts, making it virtually impossible to reassemble anything as delicate and intricate as beaded necklaces and textiles. Enamel fixative could be poured over the burial, but archaeologists wouldn't be able to separate the individual pieces without severe damage.

As he had earlier, Alva told Lucho that help would arrive, something that Alva himself had begun to doubt because the museum hadn't been able to make its last two food-and-supply deliveries. Nor had a messenger sent to summon more police been heard from. Like a commander about to send his troops into battle, Alva ordered his men to "hold the line" and "put up the appearance" that they had no more fear of the huaqueros than the huaqueros had of them.

Regardless of the impending hostilities, excavation continued from sunrise to sunset as Alva and Lucho took an overall inventory of the coffin's contents and estimated the scope of the task at hand. By this time, July 9, 1987, almost everywhere Alva looked he could see the symbols of Moche power that, until then, had existed only in his imagination or as iconographic detail in Donnan's books.

A pair of gold eyes, a gold nose, a gold mouth, and a gold chin-and-cheek visor covered the skeleton's shattered skull like a Halloween mask: part of a now decomposed shroud that Alva believed had been placed over the head and neck of the Moche lord. A gold saucer-shaped headrest cradled the cranial fragments; beneath these, like a giant flattened clam shell, lay a one-pound crescent-shaped headdress ornament of hammered gold, so large that it seemed to fill the coffin.

Matching gold nose rings, each apparently depicting a different cycle of the moon, lay stacked in descending order, much as they might have been placed on some kind of ancient lunar calendar. To Alva, this was the first unmistakable proof of the importance of the moon to this culture, and the first evidence directly linking it to a lord and ruler of the culture. Multiple sets of these moon-shaped nose rings, ranging in size from that of a bottle top to that of a large dinner plate, also indicated that the ornaments, clothing, and jewelry covering the lord were not intended to be worn all at once. Rather, these artifacts represented the lord's complete ceremonial wardrobe: key elements of uniforms that the lord wore during various ceremonies that were presumably conducted to correspond to a different phase of the moon.

Ear ornaments inlaid with turquoise depicted a Muscovy duck, probably raised for food and eaten by royalty. Moche artists stylized these ducks by turning the bill 90 degrees, so that it paralleled the rest of the bird's profile. A similar ornament portrayed a deer, now rare in the region, also associated with Moche royalty.

Around the lord's neck hung sixteen gold disks, as large as silver dollars. Perfectly round, they gleamed like miniature suns. Holes in the disks had been enlarged, as by a cord, indicating that the necklace had been worn regularly and not simply for occasional ritual display. Signs of wear identified other everyday items, including clamshell-like tweezers for plucking whiskers.

No such use marked the copper sandals Alva discovered on the lord's feet. Strictly ceremonial wear, they were impossibly stiff for comfortable walking. Not that it mattered; like Inca rulers, Moche sovereigns were often borne on litters.

The paraphernalia of high rank seemed endless. Three more headdresses could be seen under the body—one large crescent and two conical caps of cane fiber that were stitched with fine cotton thread and mounted with filigreed roundels of gilded copper. Sediments in the coffin bore traces of feathers that once adorned the headdress ornaments.

Hundreds of minute gold and turquoise beads told of

elegant bracelets. Thousands of cream, coral, and red-colored shell beads formed smock-like pectoral coverings. Five of these coverings draped the chest and shoulders of the lord. Two rested atop his legs. Four more lay beneath his skeleton. And all presented a problem never before encountered in archaeology. With more than one hundred thousand beads, each arranged to fit into a particular pattern or grouped together in shell containers, excavators could spend months, perhaps years, taking them from the coffin for later reassembly at the museum. Instead, Alva and Lucho had to develop their own technique of gluing a thick coating of cotton to the backs of the beads, and removing entire sheets of them at once, for later reassembly back at the museum.

Placement of these beads, like everything else in the tomb, must have been governed by a keen sense of balance. An eerie sense of this crept over Alva as he lifted a pair of necklaces out of the coffin. These identical strings each held ten larger-than-life peanuts, similar to the ones the police had seized from the Bernals. Five peanuts in each of the necklaces were of gold and all lay upon the lord's right side; matching silver peanuts lay to the left. Paralleling this, an ingot of gold nestled amid the bones of his right hand, an ingot of silver in his left. As Alva gradually came to learn, almost all the gold placed on top of the lord in the coffin had been laid out on his right side, while silver covered the left side. Just the reverse was true of the silver and gold laid beneath the lord's body.

A grisly clue to the lord's importance lay in his right hand, from which Alva picked up a long rattle with a gold chamber that resembled an inverted pyramid, identical to the one Donnan had shown him from Enrico Poli's collection. Its copper handle was sculptured with shields and battle clubs and terminated in a wicked-looking blade, similar to that of a scalpel. Depicted in relief on the rattle were scenes all too familiar to Alva, for Donnan had pointed them out to him in illustrations from Moche Art and Iconography. In one scene, a man wore what Alva now considered the customary regalia of the Moche lord: huge moon-shaped headdress, ear spools and nose ring, layers upon layers of beads, rattles around his waist, a woven apron, and copper sandals. Also in the scene on the rattle was a Moche lord holding a hapless prisoner by the hair and pitilessly swinging a war club at his head, evoking the initial stages of the sacrifice ceremony. Alva put the rattle back into its place in the right hand of the Moche lord with the certain knowledge that this man had known all too well how to wield this symbol of rank.

All that seemed to be missing was the goblet used to collect the prisoner's blood. But the search for this would have to wait because police had sounded the alarm.

A barrage of bottles crashed over the site, followed by gunshots, prompting Alva to throw himself over the top of the burial to protect it from broken glass. Villagers had begun to storm the site, and in response, two lone policemen had launched the first of the tear-gas canisters in an attempt to hold back the crowds.

20

Help had not arrived. Frightened police had resorted to firing one canister of tear gas after another to repel a crowd that had swelled to nearly three hundred. As the smoke cleared that morning, July 11, 1987, and angry townspeople sought temporary refuge in the cover of the sugarcane fields, Alva made the most bold and controversial decision of his career.

In full sight of the villagers, Alva asked all eighteen laborers and student excavators to gather into a tight semicircle around the royal burial chamber, a section of the pyramid that had been transformed from the pitted mass of clay bricks that it had been three months earlier to a bulwark of sandbags and trenches in the shadow of the lookout station. Alva's choice not to hold the meeting in the tent camp on the northern section of the platform was as much for their own safety as it was a means to focus on the real subject at hand: protecting the burial chamber until it could be excavated.

His men anticipated Alva asking them to join the police on the firing line. That much seemed certain, because the crowds massing in the fields had come armed with picks and shovels, garden hoes and tire irons. A few had pistols. Excavators had less than another day or two before the rioters mustered their courage and attempted another assault. And this time, Mondragon's two policemen would be called on to use submachine guns, not tear-gas launchers.

Despite long, sleepless nights, Alva showed little or no sign of the sheer exhaustion he must have felt. He looked confident and energetic, much the same man who had taken control of the site months before, and who was prepared to hold on to it now. How he found the fortitude to pull himself together at that moment remained a matter of speculation. But those closest to him said he acted out of a sudden realization that if he didn't take control of the situation, the shooting at the Bernal house would be little more than a prelude to the shootings about to take place.

Alva apologized to his teammates for putting them in danger. Until recently, he explained, his fascination with the tomb had blinded him to how precarious their position had become. He had once believed the problem would resolve itself. Instead, it had become more perilous. To ensure their safety, he now encouraged anyone who wished to leave the excavation to do so without delay.

Juan Martinez, a student archaeologist, later admitted how close he came to deserting Alva. His decision to remain at the site was less a matter of commitment to the excavation than fear of what villagers would do to him if he did leave. Ever since the beginning of July, when the first conclusive evidence of a burial chamber became apparent, Huaca Rajada's only exit had been blocked by rows of people two and three deep. Escaping at night was too dangerous because there was always one or two huaqueros patrolling the perimeter. Even if he had escaped the site itself, he had no transportation away from the village. Given the number of villagers who would recognize his face, his odds for a clean break weren't high.

Martinez wasn't the only excavator to seriously consider leaving. Montessa, Max, and Domingo had discussed the matter the night before, and chose to turn the final decision over to Lucho, long regarded as the most outspoken proponent of a full-scale evacuation, and someone who invited their candid opinions and grievances. Unlike Alva, Lucho knew their families, settled disputes, and, on Friday nights, purchased the *chicha*, or corn beer, that Mrs. Zapata and her neighbors made in great vats. His decision to remain at the site or pull out determined their choice in the matter.

Lucho had plenty of good reasons to leave. But he had one compelling to reason to stay.

Unbeknown to Alva, Lucho had begun a clandestine relationship with Maria Fuentes, a young girl who sometimes helped prepare meals at the camp. In the spirit of Romeo and Juliet, Lucho's allegiance had always been to his fellow excavators, and Maria's was to her family in the village, many of whom were poised at the entrance to Huaca Rajada with rocks in their hands. Lucho and Maria's love had blossomed in this hostile environment, and she became pregnant.

If Lucho considered collecting his belongings from his tent or talking Maria into leaving her home and returning with him to the Bruning Museum, he made no mention of it to Montessa or his men. In a show of solidarity, Lucho told the men gathered on the top of the platform that it would be a mistake to leave, "come what may."

After having obtained the support of all eighteen students and laborers, Alva admitted to making a colossal mistake in the shortsighted approach he had taken at the site. Max Diaz had taught him to be patient, not to rush an excavation. But he had also taught Alva something he believed should be as important to an archaeologist as the Hippocratic oath was to a doctor: to use the artifacts of the past to enhance man's appreciation of the present.

By excavating Huaca Rajada, Alva had tried to preserve the past. But he had done so at the expense of those who stood the most to gain. Police investigators, guns, and armed escorts could not ultimately protect Huaca Rajada if the people it belonged to wished to have it plundered.

To make amends, Alva had decided not to carve a trench around the burial and lift it out of the chamber, or to permit the police or anyone else to open fire on the crowd. Instead, he had decided to invite villagers "to see the burial for themselves."

Exactly what Alva meant by this remark, or how he intended to accomplish this task without the coffin being sacked of its treasures, he never said. Not until the next morning, July 12, when Alva approached the townspeople, did fellow excavators realize that Alva truly planned to extend his invitation to everyone, including Alberto Jaime, his most outspoken critic.

That morning, just after sunrise, a rock hit Alva in the shoulder as he walked straight past the tents built on the northern side of the platform. Undaunted, he kept coming down the clay-brick path, until he stood face-to-face with Jaime and the others, at that moment threatening him with their fists.

A space cleared around Jaime. For what must have seemed like a brief minute or two the shouting stopped, apparently out of surprise at seeing the source of their anger appear in person before them.

Reporters were not present to record what Alva said to Jaime. In the heat of the moment, Alva and the villagers all had different versions of exactly what transpired. But Alva's message was clear to everyone. Jaime's "inheritance" was waiting for him at the top of the pyramid platform. He should "help himself" before anyone "stole it" from him.

In front of the villagers' astonished eyes, Alva pulled a pair of wire cutters out of his pants pocket and snipped the three strands of barbed wire that separated himself and Jaime. Then he grabbed the protester by his collar and started to pull him up the path toward the platform.

Puzzled villagers closed ranks behind the two men, squeezing through the bottleneck where the wire had been cut. Jaime shouted for Alva to take his hands off him, but Alva kept hold until he had pulled Jaime past the tent camp and into the circle of stunned excavators.

Alva let go of Jaime at the top of the platform, inches from the opening to the burial chamber. Villagers stood shoulder-to-shoulder with the excavators, wondering what would happen next.

Jaime was left speechless for the first time anyone could remember. At least three or four inches taller than Alva, Jaime stood looking over the archaeologist's shoulder, peering down at the exposed artifacts for the first time. Alva pushed a shovel into his hands, daring Jaime to "steal from his ancestors," and "to sack his father's sacred tomb."

Alva pointed to the grave, speaking to Jaime in the same terms he spoke to schoolchildren who came for tours of the Bruning.

A "great lord of the Moche civilization," Alva proclaimed, had once made his "headquarters" right in their community, in a temple on top of this pyramid, from which he ruled a kingdom that stretched farther than the eye could see.

Before Jaime had a chance to interrupt or put the shovel down, Alva reached into the burial chamber and plucked out a giant golden bead shaped to form a human head, something that was clearly larger than anything Jaime or the other villagers had ever seen. "His people dressed him in gold," Alva shouted, handing the bead to Jaime. "Nothing less was good enough for the exalted Lord of Sipan."

Until now, no one had ever associated a name with this burial, nor had anyone handled its contents in such a cavalier manner. But doing so proved to be a brilliant decision. Referring to the burial as the "Lord of Sipan" personalized the coffin's contents. Instead of a storeroom of gold, villagers had an esteemed ancestor.

Every villager who looked into the burial chamber became transfixed, or, as a Lima journalist later referred to the phenomenon, "intoxicated by its magic." And in their intoxication, Alva learned a fundamental truth about the purpose of the Lord of Sipan's golden uniform. Artists had produced the mysterious giant beads and other ornaments to nonverbally communicate the power and magic of the Moche lord. More than two thousand years later, the ornaments had the same effect.

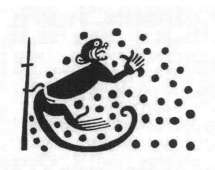

21

As hundreds of villagers crowded up the narrow path at Huaca Rajada to see the "miracle" of the Lord of Sipan, United States Customs agent Gaston Wallace, stationed at the regional headquarters in Oxnard, California, received an urgent telephone call from a nervous young man with a British accent. Michael Kelly, as the caller introduced himself, told Wallace that he had become part of an international team of professional art smugglers bringing pre-Columbian gold and ceramics plundered from Peru into Los Angeles. Wallace agreed to meet Kelly that same afternoon, September 18, 1987, on the ocean promenade in front of the Holiday Inn in nearby Ventura.

Another agent might have hesitated before giving Kelly priority treatment, but not Wallace. A handsome, clean-cut fourteen-year veteran of the Customs Service, Wallace had been fascinated by pre-Columbian art since he was a young seminarian in a small city in the Midwest. As a case officer stationed in Washington, D.C., Wallace had handled three out of the department's six major pre-Columbian investigations. Now, although the majority of his current cases involved marine interdictions, Wallace had the knowledge and expertise to realize the serious nature of Kelly's call.

Wallace met Kelly at their prearranged meeting place, a park bench overlooking the pastel-blue waters of the Pacific Ocean and the powder-white shores of the Channel Islands, just across the Ventura harbor. Despite the serene and informal setting, tension soon developed between the two men. Kelly believed that he was doing Customs a favor by informing on his associates and couldn't understand why Wallace was questioning him like a criminal. Nor could Kelly understand why Wallace was unable to grant him immunity from prosecution or offer him assurance that he would not be deported back to Britain. As Wallace explained to Kelly at that first meeting, he was only there to listen to his story and ask him questions.

Listen Wallace did, for Kelly's story couldn't be told in one meeting on the ocean promenade or even in their next meeting in Wallace's car parked under a palm tree along Channel Islands Boulevard. Back at headquarters, Kelly became a confidential witness in a case that soon eclipsed any pre-Columbian investigation in United States history; and though Kelly allegedly held back details concerning previous business activities he may have been engaged in in England, he had a spectacular talent for remembering names and dates, as well as for identifying individual artifacts in the homes or galleries of co-conspirators.

As Kelly would relate the story to Wallace and other agents, his involvement in the smuggling operation began in the summer of 1984, when he accompanied pre-Columbian antiquities collector Augusto Lodi to meet David Swetnam at the Azoff residence at 680 Picacho

Lane, Montecito. According to Kelly, Swetnam was impressed with Kelly because he had helped to arrange a ten-thousand-dollar sale, and Kelly was impressed with Swetnam because of his dynamic personality and the vast inventory of pre-Columbian objects at his sumptuous home. He and Swetnam became friends when Kelly helped to arrange Swetnam's wedding, a sunny, festive affair in Camarillo in which the bride and groom wore white and black leather. Swetnam began collecting ethnic art for Kelly on his trips to Bolivia and Peru, and in 1985, arranged for Kelly to set up his own show of contemporary Latin American painting at the Ethnos Gallery.

During the next two years, Kelly and Swetnam saw each other frequently, often at a Peruvian restaurant called Papagallo's on De la Guerra Plaza, a mecca for the Santa Barbara social set. At "smuggler's cove," as Kelly referred to Papagallo's, Swetnam introduced Kelly to a vast array of colorful individuals that included drug runners, a reputed ex-CIA hit man, convicted embezzlers, and millionaire jet-setters summering in nearby Montecito. While drinking Pisco sours, made with a fiery liquor brewed in southern Peru, Swetnam would show off the latest photographs of pre-Columbian artifacts available in Peru and boast about his success smuggling art into the United States. One particularly successful method Swetnam described consisted of covering ceramic artifacts with a cream-colored clay slip and painting them to look like contemporary pots made by the Amazonian Shipibo Indians. Kelly himself witnessed Swetnam kneeling beside a bathtub in the Azoff residence as he washed away the clay slip from the sides of one pot to reveal a three-thousand-year-old masterpiece inside.

Prior to 1986, Kelly claimed not to have considered joining Swetnam's illegal operation. But then, with his father's death and his growing financial problems, he became more and more dependent upon Swetnam. Never had this been more true than in February 1987, when Kelly and three partners joined Miguel Berckemeyer in an ill-fated deal to import colonial furniture from Lima to Los Angeles.

The importation of the furniture had begun as a strictly legal business transaction. The idea was that Kelly and his three investors would purchase furniture from the Berckemeyer family in Lima for forty thousand dollars, to be sold in the United States for a 50 percent profit. But once Kelly and the investors visited the Lima warehouse where the Berckemeyer family kept their antique furniture, arguments about the quality of the merchandise arose and the deal soured. Berckemeyer lost his temper, threatening to have the buyers detained and strip-searched at the airport. As a result, the investment group declined to put their money into furniture. Kelly was left in Lima to fend for himself, with little cash and practically no contacts. To recoup money already spent and extricate himself from an awkward predicament, Kelly approached Swetnam, offering to put up his rare collection of ethnic Mexican masks as collateral to join his smuggling operation. At the time, Kelly said, he had no idea how deeply he was going to get involved.

Wallace pressed Kelly to tell him details about Swetnam's clients. Kelly responded by revealing a side of the antiquities trade rarely seen by Customs officials. Swetnam's life, as Kelly described it, was like something out of the television show Fantasy Island, in which Swetnam jetted among exotic locales in Peru, Europe, and the United States. The luxurious compound where Swetnam entertained his clients had a swimming pool, tennis court, library, sitting room, and greenhouse. Compliments of Fred Drew, Swetnam's pet dogs were hairless Peruvian viringos. Film producer Jon Peters, who lived next door, kept a flock of penguins in his backyard.

Many of Swetnam's customers, Kelly told Wallace, were California aristocracy: Hollywood film producers, Los Angeles real estate developers, Silicon Valley computer designers, Beverly Hills decorators, and Orange County bank executives. Like these clients, Kelly had virtually been swept off his feet by Swetnam's sumptuous buffets and poolside cocktails. After all, image was often more important to many of his clients than the antiquities themselves. A rich bank executive would rather pay twelve thousand dollars for a portrait-head vase from someone driving a Jaguar convertible than two hundred dollars for the same piece with the same documentation from a salesman driving a Honda.

Kelly described Swetnam's clients as "addicted to pre-Columbian artifacts." One such client, Charles Craig, a reclusive bank executive, now retired, bought virtually anything Swetnam showed him. Another's "lust" for the antiquities resulted in his divorce and the subsequent loss of his home. Murray Gell-Mann, the Cal-Tech physicist, would sit for hours in the living room of his Pasadena home contemplating each new addition to his growing collection. All of these people, Kelly claimed, considered themselves "historians" and "connoisseurs of high culture," rationalizing their purchases with specious arguments and a sanitized, postcard vision of Latin America.

As Kelly became a greater part of the smuggling operation, he gradually grew to view his partner as little more than a sophisticated fraud and charlatan, someone who would do anything to make a sale or endear himself to a wealthy client. According to Kelly, Swetnam let his customers believe that he actually owned the mansion he entertained them in, when in fact he hadn't even met the real owner, Irving Azoff. Nor did he pay rent. Jacquelyn was actually Azoff s former maid, who had taken up residence in the servant's quarters in return for keeping an eye on the property while Azoff was at his primary residence in Beverly Hills. Azoff had no idea that Jacquelyn and her husband had taken over the main house and were using it as their own.

When clients were not around, Swetnam referred to his north-coast contacts as "dirty little Peruvians," undeserving of their vast artistic legacy. Swetnam never used his own money to buy antiquities but called on a loose syndicate of investors to front the money and assume the risk. And he had used Kelly to make his biggest deal of all: to import the Sipan treasure.

According to Kelly, at the very moment when he and Wallace were sitting on the ocean promenade, Swetnam was in Peru with Miguel Berckemeyer competing for the last remaining artifacts to have come out of the tomb. The value of the last shipment, Kelly told Wallace, amounted to more than he had ever imagined.

"It pressed a button inside me," Kelly said. "This has got to stop," he allegedly told himself.

Wallace knew that informants could be counted on to embellish their tales of trickery and deceit, but Kelly carried with him proof: two gold-and-amethyst necklaces. Besides, his story about pre-Columbian junkies on the American Riviera had a ring of truth that couldn't be ignored. In California, as in New York, London, and Tokyo, antiquities smuggling had become the younger brother of the cocaine trade, employing its own pushers, middlemen, and addicted customers. Ironically, the same rich soils of Peru, Colombia, and Bolivia that produced the coca leaf also produced much of the ancient art illegally pouring across the border. The United States had seen such an explosion of illegal art smuggling that it had become one of the most abused Customs violations, second only to narcotics. And lately, Customs inspectors had been finding that the two traveled together.

Any apprehensions Wallace may have had about Kelly were removed when he checked the Treasury Enforcement computer system and linked David Swetnam's name to a 1985 investigation involving importation of cocaine suspected of being hidden in pre-Columbian artifacts illegally smuggled into Vancouver. United States and Canadian Customs agents had raided two homes and seized one shipment containing fifty-nine antiquities. But before investigators could make arrests or track two previous shipments back to their source in Bolivia, Swetnam and his associates had abandoned their smuggling route.

Based on Kelly's testimony and the evidence compiled in Vancouver, Wallace initiated an immediate investigation. He also agreed to see what could be done to grant his informant immunity from prosecution, taking into consideration the fact that United States Customs agents and federal attorneys had never before encountered an antiquities case that crossed so many borders, involved such a varied cast of participants, and encompassed hundreds of thousands of dollars of pre-Columbian antiquities.

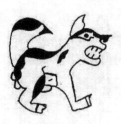

22

Newspapers and television reporters covering the events at Huaca Rajada had mixed reactions to the unusual approach Alva had taken to secure the excavation site. Alva's critics, among them a former classmate and associate at the INC in Lima, claimed that Alva's open invitation for villagers to view the Moche treasure amounted to little more than a "cheap public relations trick" at the expense of accepted archaeological operating procedures and the security of excavation personnel. Alva's supporters, on the other hand, many of them friends of the Bruning Museum or representatives of the local press, viewed his actions as a "brilliant" tactical maneuver, a "return to the bold leadership" that had permitted him to establish an excavation at Huaca Rajada in the first place.

No one in public or private, however, could dispute Alva's success. By permitting villagers to see the excavators at work, and by explaining exactly what it was that the archaeologists wanted to accomplish, Alva diffused the tensions between the two parties. Instead of posing a threat, many villagers sought to protect Huaca Rajada, and became, as one reporter called them, "a human shield" against terrorists. Tensions still existed, and attempts by Pipa and the Bernal brothers to reclaim the site still occurred, but the situation was no longer volatile. Hundreds of visitors would become a thousand, and the line of people waiting their turn to see the "shrine" at Sipan stretched from the base of the pyramid platform for almost half a mile. Never before in the history of archaeology had so many people shared in the miracle of scientific discovery that took place at Huaca Rajada between July and August 1987.

But of all the visitors who made the pilgrimage, the one Alva was most grateful to see was Christopher Donnan, the man who had been responsible for helping to keep the excavation together during those first crucial months, and the most qualified archaeologist to examine the artifacts that Lucho and Alva had removed from the tomb. Although Donnan had his hands full supervising the summer season of his own excavation at Pacatnamu, he made it a point of becoming Huaca Rajada's most regular visitor, and its most steadfast supporter in the archaeological community.

As was Donnan's custom, he would stop working at his own excavation around one-thirty P.M., climb into his Chevrolet pickup truck, and make the hour-and-a-half drive to Sipan. By this time, Alva and his excavators would have wrapped up their afternoon work so that Alva and Donnan could take stock in the progress that had been made and discuss future plans for the site.

Donnan's primary objective was to compare the inventory of objects from the Lord of Sipan's tomb with those worn by individuals depicted in Moche art and iconography. In this endeavor, Donnan reaped almost instant rewards, because virtually every artifact that Alva and his men unearthed in the tomb could be found in some form on a Moche ceramic. Donnan would often pull out a pen-and-ink drawing of the sacrifice ceremony to identify particular items, or suggest what Alva and Lucho would be finding in the tomb next.

Prominent examples of burial goods that commonly appeared in Moche art were crescent-shaped headdress ornaments, gold back flaps, cutting blades, and elaborate sets of ear ornaments. A copper pin, about six inches long, still affixed to the base of the headdress, testified to the fact that a leather or fabric band had once been used to hold the enormous sheet of hammered gold on to the head of the Lord of Sipan. Holes cut into the back flaps and cutting blades reaffirmed that these ornaments were hung on some kind of strap, perhaps a belt around the lord's waist.

Archaeologists had studied countless examples of similar royal regalia depicted on Moche stirrup-spout vases, but never before had they found a tomb that contained the actual artifacts. There was one important difference, however. From the Pacatnamu and the Viru Valley excavations, archaeologists had long assumed that items such as headdresses, back flaps, weapons, and scepters were made of carved wood, fabric, or hammered copper. Burial possessions at Huaca Rajada were made of gold and silver as well as wood, fabric, and copper.

Alva thought of a number of reasons to account for the preponderance of precious metals in the tomb. Foremost in his mind was the access that the Moche had to mines in the foothills of the Andes, especially those in the far north, in modern-day Ecuador. Archaeologists took it for granted that the farther north a culture reached, the more access it had to gold. At Huaca Rajada, one of the northern outposts of the Moche civilization, the laws of trade made it seem natural that their artists and craftsmen would have greater quantities of gold and silver to work with than at settlements farther south.

Besides the presence of large quantities of gold in the tomb, Alva and Donnan became fascinated by the advanced technological skills that Moche craftsmen and metallurgists must have employed to produce them. In this area of research, as in Moche iconography, Donnan was an expert, having published in *Archaeology* magazine the first documentary evidence of a technique that he believed the Moche culture had used to smelt metals. Based on molded-clay representations on a ceramic bowl, Donnan had portrayed how Moche craftsmen forced drafts of air into brick furnaces by means of copper or cane blowpipes, achieving temperatures of 1,300°C or higher.

Donnan had also documented how Moche craftsmen were highly skilled at hammering metal into sheets of uniform thickness, then pounding these to create objects in low relief. Hammered-metal sheets could then be joined together by edge-welding and crimping to create three-dimensional sculptures. By heating small amounts of copper oxide in a reducing atmosphere, Moche craftsmen were also skilled in reduction smelting of oxide ores, melting of copper and silver, and gold casting in closed molds.

Moche craftsmen at Huaca Rajada had used all of these previously recognized skills, and one more. Many objects that first appeared to be solid gold turned out to be gold-plated, or gilded, and objects that appeared to be solid copper bore traces of silver or gold that had once covered them. In fact, almost all of the approximately 175 metal objects in the Lord of Sipan's tomb that were not made of solid gold or silver showed signs that they had once been gilded. Prior to Alva's excavation, Donnan had seen isolated instances in which a Moche object appeared to be gilded, but he could not be certain because these objects had never been excavated in a scientific setting. Nor had Donnan ever had so many individual examples available to examine.

Heather Lechtman, of the Massachusetts Institute of Technology, helped Moche scholars to answer the perplexing question of how the Moche might have accomplished this sophisticated metallurgical technique. Using regionally available corrosive minerals, such as ordinary salt and potassium nitrate, Lechtman succeeded in gold-plating copper pennies just as Moche artisans might have gilded the moon-shaped copper rattles.

Metalworkers first dissolved gold in a solution of water and corrosive minerals, to which they added bicarbonate of soda. A clean copper object dipped into this solution served as both anode and cathode, much like a car battery. As the electric current was maintained in the bicarbonate bath and the solution gently boiled, a microscopically thin coating of gold formed on the surface of the object, giving it the appearance of pure gold. A permanent bond could later be obtained by placing the object in a kiln.

Ironically, the great artistry and technological sophistication that produced Huaca Rajada's gilded treasures had vanished along with the Moche, only to have been rediscovered hundreds of years later by Alva and his men. More discoveries were bound to be made because no scientist in Andean archaeology had ever had an opportunity to excavate a site so intimately related to the elite class of a culture as old as the Moche. As both Alva and Donnan knew, however, an ongoing excavation couldn't possibly be funded through Peruvian endowments; nor could the Bruning Museum's traditional supporters be counted on to increase their donations.

Donnan would once again offer to come to the rescue, promising on August 8, 1987, to personally raise all the money Alva would need and to see that his crew was well staffed. But as relieved as Alva was to hear this, and as pleased as Donnan was to use his influence to help his colleague at this important juncture in his career, their enthusiasm to excavate was soon tempered by unforeseen obstacles.

In the course of Gaston Wallace's investigation, Customs agents had contacted Donnan and asked if he would assist in what they merely described as a "pre-Columbian smuggling investigation." As a matter of policy, Donnan politely declined their request, not realizing until months later that doing so had put him on the horns of a thorny ethical dilemma. The same highly placed contacts whom Donnan counted on to keep him informed of recently unearthed Moche artifacts turned out to be the people Customs agents sought the most information about.

Donnan had long made it a practice to keep his eye out for any Moche artifacts that might surface in private collections, and made no secret of his visits to the homes of important pre- Columbian antiquities collectors and dealers to obtain photographs for his Moche archive. By paying regular visits to the homes of these dealers and collectors and assuring them of his discretion, Donnan was permitted to photograph Moche artifacts that archaeologists might not have otherwise known about. His motivation was quite clear: to benefit current and future Moche scholarship.

United States Customs agents took a less pragmatic view. Photographing artifacts illegally smuggled out of Peru reflected complicity and encouraged further criminal behavior by establishing the authenticity of a particular artifact and thus enhancing its market value. Not only had Donnan photographed looted Huaca Rajada antiquities, but he had done so at the invitation of Fred Drew and David Swetnam, the ringleaders for the entire smuggling operation. And what agents had most recently learned, but not revealed to Donnan, was that David Swetnam and Miguel Berckemeyer had returned to Peru and taken up residence at the Hotel de Turistas in Chiclayo, less than an hour's drive from Alva's excavation. INC officials in Lima and Chiclayo were alerted to their presence and had them followed. Anyone who met with them, including Donnan, became a suspect.

Alva's activities also came under scrutiny for his having arrived at Huaca Rajada under the premise of conducting a "salvage" operation, not an "excavation." INC officials, sensitive to the unusual amount of activity at the site in the wake of Ernil's shooting, had dispatched an investigator to look into Alva's operation and return with any artifacts seized by the police. At that time, almost three months earlier, Lucho and Alva had teamed up to keep the investigator drunk. Lucho and Alva were so successful in this endeavor that the INC investigator didn't set foot outside the Bruning Museum for his entire two-day visit. He left unaware that anything had been found at the site besides a few gold beads.

Alva now faced a more complex and sinister problem. He couldn't begin to hide a full-scale excavation from his superiors. Nor could he protect the precarious alliance he had made with the villagers. By inviting them onto the site to view the tomb, and in one case handle actual artifacts, Alva had disregarded INC protocol and operating procedures. At best, Alva could expect an official inquiry into his actions. More likely, however, Francisco Iriarte, director of archaeology for the INC in Lima, and a man who had already tried to take official credit for the discoveries at the site, would transfer Lucho to Trujillo, send Alva back to the Bruning Museum, and assign himself the official responsibility of supervising the excavation.

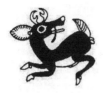

23

True to his promise, Donnan began the formidable task of raising money for Alva's excavation. An emergency grant engineered by archaeologist James Richardson through the Heinz Foundation provided an immediate $8,000; two weeks later, in Washington, D.C., Donnan applied for and received $43,000 from the National Geographic Society for the first year of excavation and another $49,000 for the second year: the most significant funding ever provided an archaeological project supervised by a Peruvian national. In a rare personal appearance before the Research Committee, Donnan presented the first 35-mm slides showing the contents of the tomb of the Lord of Sipan. Another grant, arranged through the Bruning Museum sponsors in Mainz, Germany, provided an additional $2.5 million in technical assistance for the proper care and restoration of the artifacts once they were excavated.

Donnan also devised a plan to protect Alva's tenuous position as director of archaeology at the site. In his capacity as one of the administrators of the National Geographic grants, Donnan attached a proviso that named the Bruning Museum as the direct recipient of the funding, not the Department of Archaeology of the INC. Angered by the new development, Francisco Iriarte vehemently protested the unusual dispersal of funds directly to the Bruning and not through his office in Lima. But he had no one to complain to because Donnan made it clear that Huaca Rajada would receive no funding unless Alva was in charge. Moreover, all grant payments were spread out over a period of twenty-four months and sent directly from UCLA to the Bruning Museum by personal messenger, thus eliminating any unnecessary delays in transit and preventing anyone in the INC or the Peruvian government from levying an "administrative" tax on the funding once it reached Peru.

Besides political and financial protection, Donnan also lent equipment, time, and expertise to Alva's excavation, including the unique pool of international talent that he had assembled at Pacatnamu. In this way, Dr. John Verano, Donnan's UCLA-trained physical anthropologist, became the first of the Pacatnamu excavators to join Alva and his men, and the only non-Peruvian besides Donnan to play a significant on-the- site role at Huaca Rajada.

Born in Austria and raised in California, thirty-two-year-old Verano had spent a precocious childhood collecting fossils and bones from around the world, a collection he treated with the same enthusiasm and profound interest with which his childhood companions regarded their prized collections of baseball cards. He soon translated his adolescent fascination into a professional career as a physical anthropologist, an occupation that brought him international attention in 1985 when he excavated a lurid collection of fourteen mutilated bodies buried at a Chimu ceremonial complex at Pacatnamu. Ranging in age from fifteen to thirty-five, some of the bodies had been beheaded; others had lost limbs or been impaled on spears, their naked bodies exposed to vultures and left in the sand to rot.

Verano's specialty, however, was not the Chimu but the Moche, which made his skills as an anthropologist all the more valuable to Alva and his excavation team. In fact, Verano's previous research at Pacatnamu was as crucial to a proper understanding of the skeletal remains unearthed at Huaca Rajada as Donnan's iconographic research was to understanding the significance of the burial possessions.

At Pacatnamu, the majority of Moche skeletal collections Verano studied related to the final phase of the Moche kingdom, or Moche V, dated approximately A.D. 500—750, a period two hundred years after the burial of the Lord of Sipan. The skeletal examples that were recovered comprised 65 burials excavated from a single cemetery, 26 burials from other parts of the site, and approximately 590 specimens from three large Moche cemeteries plundered by looters. Based on the distribution of the corpses buried in the cemeteries, Verano determined that the probability of death was consistent with a U-shaped mortality curve common with contemporary populations on Peru's north coast. Most people who survived childhood died between ages twenty-five and forty-nine, although females tended to live significantly longer than males. Whether this was due to greater violence or more hazardous activities among men, or to greater susceptibility of males to disease, Verano didn't know. But in spite of the frequent portrayals of warfare, capture, and sacrifice depicted on Moche ceramics, Verano found little evidence of fractures, wounds, or other injuries, which provided further evidence that the Moche confined conflict to ritual settings.

Verano also learned that the Moche were not particularly tall people. Males stood approximately five feet three, and females, four feet eleven. Infants and children showed few developmental problems because of low protein or insufficient calories, and adults, though short, were strongly built. All the older individuals and several younger adults had some degree of arthritis in the joints, particularly the hips, knees, shoulders, and elbows. And, like other peoples whose diet consisted of soft foods and carbohydrates, the Moche suffered from cavities and tooth loss.

Approximately half of the Moche skulls Verano studied showed signs of having been artificially deformed, or flattened. The deformation was usually a mild to pronounced flattening of the back of the skull, with flattening of the forehead region occasionally visible as well. Broadening of the cranial vault and slight broadening of the cheeks was also noticeable in most of the deformed skulls. Verano concluded that this deformation was probably not an attempt by the Moche to alter the shape of the head for aesthetic reasons, but the unintentional result of infant cradle-boarding. Moche mothers, Verano assumed, had wrapped their children from head to foot onto wooden boards so that they could be easily carried on their backs while working in a field or with their hands.

Verano also made some startling discoveries about burial practices at Pacatnamu. Instead of one large cemetery where the Moche buried their dead, more than twenty smaller cemeteries were scattered across the site. Using standard forensic techniques, Verano determined that individuals buried in the same cemetery resembled one another more closely than they did individuals buried in other cemeteries of the same time period. Because greater resemblance implies closer genetic relationship, he interpreted the results as suggesting that the Moche buried their dead by family groups or clans.

Eager to compare his research to what was uncovered at the high-status tomb at Huaca Rajada, Verano energetically volunteered to join Donnan on his next trip to

Lambayeque.

Darkly tanned after more than a month of continuous fieldwork at Pacatnamu, the affable, blue-eyed young scholar arrived in July 1987 to familiarize himself with the excavation and to make a preliminary examination of the skeletal remains that Alva had unearthed. Verano returned on a routine basis for the next three months as more Moche treasures were removed from the burial and Alva and Lucho finally began to extract the skeleton.

Unlike the bones of the guardian, those of the Lord of Sipan couldn't be removed in a rectangular block of hardened acrylic without damaging artifacts lower down in the coffin. Alva had to painstakingly collect the bones of the Lord of Sipan's skull first, carefully placing these in a wooden box that Benedicto had specially constructed for this purpose. Alva then poured a thin coat of acrylic preservative over the remaining bones, slipped slats of wood underneath, raised the rest of the skeleton out of the burial chamber, and placed it in a second box. By this time, November 1987, Verano had spent so many hours looking at the skeletal remains over the shoulders of Lucho and the others that in January 1988, when he made a thorough examination of the skeleton, he was not surprised by what he found.

Bones of Huaca Rajada's vintage are often brittle, and the skeleton of the Lord of Sipan was largely blackened splinters. The skull consisted of more than three hundred separate shards, crushed as the timbers vaulting the coffin had slowly collapsed and the earth above blanketed the burial and its contents. By the time Alva had removed the last of the sediment from the skeleton, the only bones that remained intact were four vertebrae and two heel bones. Regardless, Verano had the pieces of a complete skeleton, a luxury considering its age and the amount of corrosive material buried alongside it.

When Verano arrived at the Bruning's examination room, his well-worn knapsack contained several cameras, a tape recorder, spiral notebooks, paintbrushes, scalpels, and his treasured collection of dental picks. Alva and Lucho carried the two wooden boxes containing the Lord of Sipan out of the museum's secured storage room and placed them on the table. Verano set to work immediately.

As in every other archaeological endeavor, the time and energy expended on preparation were as important as the time devoted to analysis. Like a three-dimensional puzzle, the hundreds of shards comprising the Lord of Sipan's skull had to be sorted and cemented together. A complete inventory of the other remains had to be logged into notebooks, measurements and photographs taken, and any signs of disease or fractured bones noted. Every scrap of bone had to be carefully examined for any clue it might reveal about its owner.

Hour after hour, Verano sat beside a jar of paraloid bone glue, a sandbox to hold the pieces while the glue dried, and several osteology and anatomy books for quick reference. Gluing the skull back together took enormous concentration and patience, particularly as the task neared completion, for the bones were very fragile and frequently came apart in his hands.

Basing his conclusions upon distinguishing characteristics of the skull and the size of the thigh and arm bones, Verano confirmed Alva's preliminary analysis that the Lord of Sipan was an adult male. The areas of muscle attachment on his bones showed he was a physically active individual with short but wide feet, approximately size 8 with a triple-E width. He stood about five and a half feet tall, or two to three inches taller than the average adult male Moche that Verano had examined at Pacatnamu.

Like his counterparts at Pacatnamu, he suffered from

mild arthritis in the vertebrae of his lower back, although it was unlikely that it gave him more than occasional discomfort. No degenerative changes were visible in the bones of his jaw, elbows, or other joints that might indicate advanced age. His full set of teeth showed no signs of disease or decay except for a small cavity in his lower-left first molar.

Also like many of his Pacatnamu counterparts, the Lord of Sipan's flattened forehead confirmed that he had probably been cradle-boarded as a child, suggesting alternative possibilities as to how the lords of the Moche kingdom may have been selected. Either the Lord of Sipan was not of royal birth, or Moche infants, regardless of lineage, were treated the same.

The absence of dental wear or other degenerative changes in the skeleton indicated that the Lord of Sipan probably died in his middle to late thirties, quite young by Pacatnamu standards. A sudden death at an early age might explain the presence of the hastily produced ceramic wares buried in the chamber above him.

How had the Lord of Sipan died?

Verano ruled out poor diet and could find no evidence suggesting either violent death or prolonged bone-damaging or deforming disease. But however the lord may have died, he departed his people prematurely. And, as Alva and Verano would soon learn, he had not gone alone.

24

An inventory of the contents of the Lord of Sipan's coffin revealed handcrafted treasures of gold and silver that were a quantum leap above those of the richest Moche tomb previously excavated. Yet the one treasure that both Alva and Donnan anticipated being unearthed failed to materialize: the goblet used to collect a prisoner's blood at the sacrifice ceremony. Now that the coffin had been emptied, Alva and Donnan assumed that the sacrificial goblet would be discovered in a hidden niche beside the burial, much as excavators had discovered the scepter in the chamber looted by huaqueros. But as Montessa and Lucho exposed the chamber floor and then began the laborious process of cleaning the soil and sediment from around the Lord of Sipan's coffin, excavators found no goblet. Instead, from late November 1987 until early February 1988, excavators unearthed the remains of six more burials, all placed in tubular cane coffins surrounding the royal coffin.

Buried at the Lord of Sipan's head were the bones of a young girl, aged approximately ten to thirteen, with her arms and legs extended. Directly underneath and parallel to her lay the bones of a second young girl, about the same age, also with arms and legs extended. A third young girl was buried at the foot of the royal coffin, also with her arms and legs extended. Unlike the two burials at the head of the coffin, the third young girl had a gilded copper headdress, suggesting a higher status, perhaps Moche royalty. All three of their skulls showed signs of artificial flattening. Otherwise their bones revealed a normal development pattern. No signs of any life-threatening disease or other ailments were found.

Head-to-head with the young girls buried at the head and foot of the coffin were the bones of two large and burly men, buried to the lord's right and left sides. Both men were approximately the same age and older than the Lord of Sipan. A copper shield, headdress, and war club indicated that the man buried to the right of the Lord of Sipan may have been a warrior or soldier. Because of a rich array of ornaments, including a gilded back flap and a cone-shaped helmet, Alva and Lucho considered him of higher status than the lord's guardian, buried above. He was probably also of higher status than the other burly man buried at the left side of the Lord of Sipan, who wore nothing besides a beaded frock. At the feet of this skeleton lay buried what appeared to be the bones of a monkey. Later analysis, however, revealed the bones to belong to a dog, most likely the Lord of Sipan's personal and prized hound, buried beside a royal servant.

A final burial was unearthed in a flexed or seated position in the southwest corner of the tomb, beside the Lord of Sipan's head. This burial was the remains of a child, approximately nine to ten years of age, its bones too decomposed to determine its sex. Like one of the burly men, this child also wore a headdress, but this headdress was more delicate than the other, consisting of a single gilded copper band embossed with the symbol of a puma. Examination of the child's teeth revealed a large lesion on one molar and multiple growth-arrest lines on other teeth, reflecting several episodes of developmental stress, either illness or dietary deficiency from which the child had recovered but which left a permanent record in the developing tooth crowns. The lesion on the molar, quite rare in other Moche skeletal samples, also reflected poor health.

With the exception of dental cavities in two of the burials, no evidence of active disease was found on any of the six skeletons. Nor was any obvious indication of injury or violent death present, although the poor condition of the skeletons would make such evidence very difficult to identify. But in spite of their severe decomposition, evidence still existed to aid in determining whether these men and women had been sacrificed for the Lord of Sipan at his funeral.

During his examination of the skeletons, Verano noted some unusual features that suggested that they may not have been buried at the same time as the Lord of Sipan. The male skeletons lay in the tomb extended on their backs, in the standard Moche burial position. It was interesting, therefore, to find that the other burials in the tomb varied from this posture. The most obvious case was that of the child, found in a flexed or seated position. But the skeletons of the three adolescent girls showed both unusual body positions and signs of disarticulation, or scattering of skeletal elements. This "scrambling," as Verano referred to it, couldn't possibly be explained by the slumping of the earth under the tomb or pressure from above. Nor could slumping of the earth or pressure from above account for a number of missing parts or amputations, for both the men buried at the Lord of Sipan's sides and the young girl buried at the foot of his coffin lacked left feet.

In the case of the three young girls, Verano noticed substantial decomposition of the soft tissues of the stomach area, along with scrambling of the ribs and vertebrae far beyond the bone scattering that would be expected in the normal course of decomposition. In the most obvious example, the pelvis of one of the young girls was rotated in the opposite direction from her head, making it virtually impossible to have positioned her body in the burial chamber without severing the spinal column or waiting for severe decomposition to have occurred. The ribs of one of the other girls were not in their natural order. Teeth were found scattered near her feet, wrist bones underneath her shoulder bone. Examination of the third young girl revealed that her left arm, shoulder, and part of the rib cage were also rotated approximately 90 degrees counterclockwise.

Verano first thought that the bodies of these young girls, perhaps wives or royal consorts, had been dismembered or cut into pieces before being placed inside their burial niches, but no clean incisions or cuts could be seen on their individual bones. Also, organic remains of their tubular cane coffins and impressions of the cane fibers on the human remains indicated that the scrambling had occurred after the bodies had been placed inside their coffins but before the coffins had begun to decompose.

Another possible solution occurred to Verano. Perhaps the partially decomposed remains of these three young girls had been moved before finally being put to rest in the Lord of Sipan's burial chamber. Given the normally dry condition of the Lambayeque Valley and its natural tendency to mummify or desiccate a corpse, it was not difficult for Verano to imagine that the three young girls were placed in individual cane coffins for a period of months, perhaps years, then exhumed and put in the burial chamber beside the Lord of Sipan.

To Alva, this meant but one thing. Much like the Egyptian practice of killing adolescent girls for later burial in the tomb of a pharaoh, the three young girls at the head and foot of the royal coffin hadn't been wives or consorts but chosen sacrifices who had been killed at various religious ceremonies long before the Lord of Sipan lost his life.

Donnan went as far as to suggest that their mummified remains could have been stored for decades in one of the small temples atop the pyramids. This may have even been the temple's sole purpose: to contain the sacred remains of sacrifices until the passage of the lord into the afterlife. A great deal of collateral evidence existed to support this hypothesis because the Inca, centuries after the Moche, kept their rulers mummified and brought their corpses out on special occasions, dressed them, offered them food, and even spoke to them. Perhaps, as Donnan suggested, venerating the dead as if they were still living was an Andean concept embraced or originated by the Moche.

Because all three of the young girls fell into a very narrow age range and showed similar patterns of disarticulation, Alva and Verano supposed that they had been sacrificed prior to the Lord of Sipan's death. Not so the two burly men buried on either side of his coffin. As previously noted, the guardian buried above the Lord of Sipan was a young adult male, appropriate in terms of age and sex for his presumed role as guard of the royal burial chamber. The two burly men, perhaps lifelong

retainers, appeared to have been older than their master, their ages compatible with their station. They were probably killed along with the dog at the time of the Lord of Sipan's funeral.

The young child in the southeast corner of the tomb could not be so easily identified. Numerous explanations for its presence occurred to Alva and Verano, two of which were that its seated position might simply reflect a lack of space in the tomb, or that its headdress and position beside the Lord of Sipan indicated a family relationship, possibly a royal child who died naturally.

Alva wondered whether he would ever know the child's true identity. But one thing boosted his morale: For the last six months he had focused all his attention on a small portion of the entire pyramid; he still had more than three quarters of the pyramid left to examine.

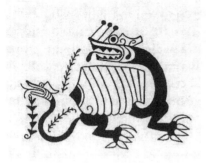

25

In the six months that elapsed since Michael Kelly had agreed to become secret United States government informant S-3 OX, Gaston Wallace's smuggling investigation had spread from Ventura to Montecito, Los Angeles to Beverly Hills, London to Lima. But even Wallace did not realize the full scope of his investigation until March 30, 1988, the morning sixty armed Customs agents launched the largest raid and seizure of pre-Columbian art in United States history.

Thirty-nine-year-old special agent Robert Casey, selected to enforce the search warrants in the Los Angeles and Santa Barbara areas, had spent almost as much time with Kelly as Wallace had. Like his chief investigator, Casey listened to nearly fifteen hours of secret tape recordings that Kelly made in the course of the investigation, and pored over photos of antiquities Kelly had taken on a trip to London. At Casey's direction, Kelly had prepared detailed maps of each of the homes or businesses to be raided, including precise locations where individual pieces would be found. The importance of this information could not be underestimated because the owners of the homes and businesses that Casey was assigned to raid were some of the most important and influential people in Southern California. Unless the raids were conducted flawlessly, United States Customs could expect a storm of lawsuits and bad publicity.

Determined to recheck every detail of the operation, Casey called the thirty officers under his immediate supervision together in an Oxnard conference room on the night before the raid. For security reasons, no one in attendance but Casey knew the real identity of informant S-3 OX, not even art consultant Dorie Reents-Budet, brought in from the University of California at Santa Barbara to help Casey prepare the most important part of his lecture: how agents could identify pre-Columbian art from the multitude of other art that they were certain to find at each location. Using the slides Kelly had taken at the Fine Art Services storage room in London, Casey was able to target specific objects for seizure.

Once the general parameters of what they were going to look for were established, Casey divided the agents into teams and assigned each member a specific duty. While one agent was responsible for searching for all the pre-Columbian antiquities at one location, another would search for the paper trail of Rolodexes, business ledgers, and canceled checks that prosecutors could later use to link the clients and dealers together. As in the case of Ben Johnson, who was known to have resold a number of significant pieces that Swetnam had provided him, it was imperative to secure as much documentary evidence as possible.

Before calling an end to the meeting, Casey outlined an unusual operations procedure. Bonded art handlers from Cookes Crating in downtown Los Angeles would arrive at each location by minivan to remove, photograph, and store any seized artifacts. Under normal circumstances, such a procedure would be deemed unnecessary, but in a situation in which agents would be handling irreplaceable two-thousand-year-old art objects, United States Attorney William Smith in Los Angeles and Laura Weddell, his co-counsel at regional headquarters in Long Beach, considered Cookes Crating indispensable.

After answering final questions, Casey ended the meeting with an order to study the documents he had handed out, then to meet the next morning at the parking lot of Carrows Restaurant, adjacent to Highway 101, halfway between Oxnard and Santa Barbara. Agents living nearby would return to their homes that night; those from Los Angeles would be staying at the local Hilton.

At six o'clock the next morning, Casey's men assembled at the Carrows parking lot as advance teams contacted local police and scouted each location for unusual developments or unforeseen activity. One by one the advance teams reported back that all was clear. Casey gave the go-ahead, then turned his own car onto 101 North to supervise the raid on the home of retired Crocker Bank executive Charles Craig, at 21 West Arrellaga Street in Santa Barbara.

Everything Casey knew about Craig's house he had learned from Michael Kelly. But unlike the other residences targeted in the raid, this house remained a mystery because Kelly had never actually been inside it. On the few occasions he had visited Craig to pick up or deliver artifacts, Kelly had only been permitted to stand on the porch. Craig was described by Kelly as a curious, reclusive individual with a reputation as a major art buyer, whether it was modern sculpture or pre-Columbian antiquities.

Just as Kelly had described, Craig's house was not the modern high-security fortress that agents had come to expect from rich art collectors. Craig lived in a decaying three-story Victorian town house, its pale-yellow paint peeling away from its gingerbread exterior, trash piled up on its open veranda, grass and weeds choking what passed for a front lawn. "The house looked haunted," Casey later recalled, comparing Craig's home to the Havisham mansion in Dickens's Great Expectations.

At the door, Casey was met by a partially clad man who appeared to be in his late seventies or early eighties. Charles Craig, as he introduced himself, was actually twenty years younger than he looked, but since he seldom left his home, and rarely permitted anyone inside besides a small circle of intimate friends, Craig no longer took the trouble to groom himself.

What surprised Casey more than anything else was the contrast between the squalid condition of the house and the magnificence of the art collection within. Nothing inside had apparently been cleaned, dusted, or repaired for years. Wallpaper peeled from its backing; dishes had sat for so long in the kitchen that the food on them was not even recognizable; dust collected on piles of old newspapers and empty beer cans. But in the midst of this was an art collection that took Casey's breath away. Paintings, statuary, carvings, and prints were everywhere: pre-Columbian art, old masters, Renaissance oils, African carvings, Roman coins, and works by the abstract expressionists.

What Casey had just begun to realize was that Charles Craig was one of the most eclectic art collectors in Southern California. His pre-Columbian collection consisted of more than twelve hundred items, including Inca headdresses from Peru, painted Mayan ceramics from

Honduras, and Aztec stone carvings from Mexico. His European art treasures included works by Jacques Villon, Auguste Rodin, Francisco Goya, and Rembrandt van Rijn. There were rare books by authors such as Sir Walter Scott, illustrations by John Leech, and modern paintings and sculpture by John McCracken, Joseph Cornell, Arshile Gorky, and Jean Arp.

Given his extraordinary art collection, Craig was anything but smug or self-important. He appeared to Casey as a gentle, good-humored older man who wished for nothing more than to make the United States Customs' job as easy as possible. Unlike some of the other collectors targeted in raids in Beverly Hills, who resented the intrusion of Customs officers into their homes, Craig helped agents to select the hundreds of pre-Columbian artifacts from the rest of his collection. Nor did he appear to be concerned when Casey seized a key to a safety-deposit box at a local bank, a rental agreement from a nearby storage room, and a set of barely legible insurance papers.

By the time Casey had found these documents, Customs agents had already begun the time-consuming process of logging and then photographing seized art. In order to best protect the objects, all photographing took place outside on the lawn under natural light. As a result, a large crowd of curious onlookers had gathered. Among them was a man standing in his bathrobe, holding a cup of coffee. "Bob," as Craig referred to him, had come out on the porch of his condominium on the corner to ask if everything was all right. Craig assured him that it was.

Casey paid scant attention to the casual exchange between the two men and went back to look for more pre-Columbian artifacts, especially those that may have come from the pyramids at Huaca Rajada. Though some 250 pieces had been gathered by two-thirty P.M., none of the seized artifacts appeared to have been part of the shipments Michael Kelly had told Wallace about. Without further delay, Casey obtained Craig's permission to check his safety-deposit box. Finding nothing but an expired insurance policy there, Casey drove over to the storage room.

Besides more oil paintings and sculptures, Casey became aware of two things when he opened the storage room: a huge puddle on the concrete floor and a large cardboard box sitting beside it. Ignoring everything else in the room, Casey went directly to the cardboard box, where he found a portion of the artifacts he had been looking for. Many were wrapped in the same Lima newspapers that had accompanied them out of Peru four months earlier. Luckily, the puddle of water and moisture in the air had not damaged the treasures.

By the time Casey and Craig returned to Arrellaga Street, the crowd had grown larger and press and television reporters were swarming around the front steps and veranda trying to get a closer look inside the house. The Santa Barbara Sheriff's Department arrived on the scene, helping Customs agents by establishing order outside, and later by making an important discovery inside.

A particularly observant sheriff noticed an unusual bulge under a sheet of old contact paper behind the refrigerator. Agents immediately removed a pile of old rugs and a stack of newspapers from in front of the refrigerator and pulled the refrigerator out. Peeling back the contact paper, agents exposed a sealed door. Behind the door was a narrow hallway. Down the hallway were two rooms closed off from the rest of the house, their windows boarded up. As was the case everywhere else in the house, art hung from the ceilings, covered the walls, and lay stacked on the floor. But here was where Craig kept his real masterpieces, including what appeared to be a pre-

Columbian altar, complete with tumi knives, burial urns, and ceremonial cups.

Casey now knew that Craig hadn't been as helpful in locating the imported artifacts in his collection as he had pretended to be: all the more reason, Casey thought, to investigate the insurance papers that had been found beside Craig's easy chair. A close examination would reveal the papers to be yellow carbons of originals filed at the Santa Barbara Museum of Art a few months earlier. To save time deciphering the carbons, Craig volunteered to call ahead to the museum to let officials know that they were coming to get a more legible copy of the original insurance forms.

In order to reach the administrative offices at the Santa Barbara Museum of Art, visitors who enter from the front first have to walk through the main exhibition galleries. Casey and Craig took this route, but paused by an exhibition hall scheduled to open in two days. Casey stopped at the entrance because he recognized the now familiar shape of a Moche pyramid painted on one of the walls. He recognized the painting, just as he recognized almost all the sculptures, ceramics, ceremonial items, and jewelry around the room, because art historian Dorie Reents-Budet had shown him pictures and slides of similar objects, and because Michael Kelly had described them to Gaston Wallace at their first meeting in Ventura.

Of approximately 274 pre-Columbian artifacts on display, Kelly had identified at least 20 that had once been in David Swetnam's inventory, and another 7 that Kelly claimed his partner had personally brought into the United States.

Among the many disturbing aspects of this discovery was the fact that Dorie Reents-Budet had written catalog copy for an exhibit of Charles Craig's collection two months prior to the raid, and that Santa Barbara Museum of Art officials reportedly began to shred the catalog to the new exhibit on the very morning customs agents seized Craig's artifacts. Casey also learned that "Bob," as Craig had referred to his neighbor on Arrellaga Street, was none other than Robert Henning, chief curator of the museum and the inspiration behind the show. Henning had also organized the earlier showing of Craig's artwork, celebrating the "passion," "imagination," and "energy" of the private collector.

It seemed inconceivable to Casey that Henning, an acknowledged expert on Craig's collection, hadn't known the true origin of the artifacts. But all Casey could say for certain was that Sipan had come to Santa Barbara in an important way. Antiquities plundered from a Peruvian tomb less than four months earlier were being exhibited in one of the most prestigious museums in the United States.

PART 5

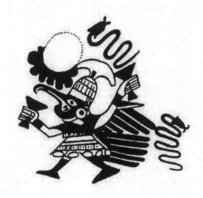

HIGH PRIEST
OF SIPAN

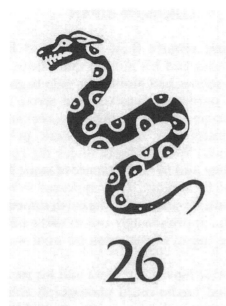

26

Before news of the police raids reached Peru, Alva would have a celebration of his own: Excavation on April 2, 1988, into a three-by-five-meter cut in the southeastern section of the platform revealed the sure signs of a second royal burial chamber. Its contents, however, remained a secret for almost a month, as Alva and Lucho made a series of startling discoveries about the use other cultures may have had for Huaca Rajada.

Montessa and his men, assigned the task of brick removal and cleaning, unearthed fourteen late-period burials in the northern section of the platform, ranging in age from the Chimu culture in the year A.D. 1100 to the early Hispanic colonial occupation in 1600. All burials were placed in shallow graves near the upper surface, and most contained one or more ceramic vessels. Lack of any gold, silver, or copper objects indicated that the burials belonged to middle-or lower-class individuals, most likely interred at Huaca Rajada after the platform had lost most of its major religious importance and may well have begun to erode into the shapeless mound huaqueros had begun to plunder.

In order to give himself and Lucho room on the platform to photograph and remove these later-period burials, Alva transferred Montessa and his men to the southern section of the platform. No sooner had Montessa's men begun to remove bricks there than once again a call echoed across the platform to summon Lucho or Alva to examine the remains of human burials. These interments, however, were pre-Moche, or Chavin, as evidenced by their depth under the core of Moche bricks on the surface and by the existence of stone masonry and other construction techniques. They appeared to be middle to upper-class individuals, placed into the earth sometime between 1000 and 200 B.C., approximately two to three hundred years before the Moche began construction on what was to become Huaca Rajada.

Once again Alva moved Montessa and his men to another area so that he and Lucho could photograph and extract the burials. Brick removal and cleaning now took place in the central portion of the platform, a few feet north of the burial chamber of the Lord of Sipan. This time, Montessa and his men unearthed the foundation of a rectangular ramp that priests or other royalty must have once used to climb to the temple or throne that Alva believed had once stood atop the platform. An examination of bricks taken from a cross-section revealed evidence of Chavin, Moche, and Chimu construction techniques.

Discovery of the ramp and burials indicated that the site had been used as a religious or ceremonial enclave for centuries before the Moche arrived and centuries after most archaeologists believed that the culture had vanished from the area. Burials that Alva had previously considered random, or "intrusive," may have been allied to the site in some spiritual or ceremonial way, just as Moche lords may have chosen to expand or renovate a preexisting Chavin ceremonial site. In this regard, Mrs. Zapata's myths and half-remembered stories about the Moche "House of the Moon" might mean that moon worship at Huaca Rajada had been the contact point connecting the various cultures, the reason for the site's continuous use for more than a thousand years.

In order to give himself and Lucho more time and space to study these new burials, Alva ordered Montessa and his men to move once more. Half the labor force began to clear the area immediately behind Mrs. Zapata's house, while the other half put aside their trowels and dustpans to begin a number of much-needed construction projects. A team headed up by Domingo built a permanent shelter to store excavation equipment and process the overwhelming mass of archaeological collections being made. A team under the direction of Maximo built Sipan's first schoolhouse, put a roof on the town hall, and improved the road leading to the site. A committee of villagers, archaeologists, and laborers, headed by village leader Pedro Ramos, took on the task of exploring other improvements that Alva and his men could make in the community at large.

While excavating the minor burials, Alva and Lucho had spent little or no time exploring the one area on the platform that held the most promise: a rectangle of small stones and fill that looked identical to the cut that had led to the burial chamber of the Lord of Sipan. A few hours after excavation began on this area, a burial was unearthed in the same position as the one in which the guardian of the previous tomb had been found. But as Alva and Lucho soon learned, this was no guardian, at least not the kind they had come to expect.

From beneath excavators' brushes emerged the bones of a small child, aged approximately ten to twelve. Decomposition made it impossible to tell the sex, reason for death, or any special characteristics, giving Alva and Lucho nothing to base their conclusions on except the curious placement of the burial, with its head to the north and feet to the south, exactly opposite more traditional Moche burials.

After excavating the fabulous cache of ceramics located next to the first tomb, Lucho and Alva expected to find something a bit more imposing than the burial of a lone child. Had this child been of royal birth, it would seem only natural that the burial contain precious metal artifacts or a headdress, or be wrapped in a royal burial shroud. If, on the other hand, this child represented some kind of sacrifice, it would seem only natural that ceramics accompany it. But no ceramics and no rich burial possessions were found. However, just as the guardian had been unearthed a foot and a half above the chamber containing the first tomb, so too the bones of this child marked the earth above a chamber that Alva and Lucho penetrated next.

Time and moisture had also taken their toll on the wooden beams covering this chamber. The timbers had long since carbonized, and there was little to see besides the discoloration of the decaying wood and the imprints of ten-foot beams that had bent under the immense weight of the earth they supported. As cleaning of this area began and scaffolding was erected, work on the rest of the site ground to a halt. A large gathering of people surrounded Lucho and Alva as they began the laborious process of brushing away the remains of the timbers, then the fine silt beneath.

Approximately four inches beneath this timbering Alva uncovered the remains of a second burial. His and Lucho's initial belief was that they had unearthed the guardian they had sought to find earlier, because the five-feet-two-inch human skeleton that took shape beneath the silt matched that of the burial directly above the coffin of the Lord of Sipan. Between the ages of sixteen and twenty-five, this adult male lay buried on his back. In his right hand was a large, rectangular copper shield, and in his left, a large ceramic ladle, or dipper. Both shield and ladle were heavily decorated in typical Moche relief: a face, half-human, half-animal, embossed on the exterior. His feet, like those of the guardian of the first tomb, were nowhere to be found. If they were surgically removed from his legs or hacked off while he was still alive, neither Alva nor Lucho could say, but the ghastly open-mouth expression of terror frozen on his face suggested the latter.

Another curious difference between this burial and that of the guardian exhumed from the previous tomb was that the Lord of Sipan's guardian had been interred at a diagonal. This body had been made on a north-south axis, suggesting a more traditional type of Moche burial. Yet the head of this figure lay to the north, his feet to the south, just the opposite of what Alva expected.

If a key existed to unlock the secret of this burial, Alva knew that it rested with the presence of the ceramic dipper in his left hand, a rare occurrence in Moche burials. Hundreds of ceramic jars, pots, and other assorted vessels had been unearthed in Moche graves, but Alva hadn't heard of a single instance of a dipper being found. Furthermore, only in Moche art had he ever seen one decorated with a carved head on its handle. Pictured on the side of a stirrup-spout in a private collection in Trujillo, the dipper was portrayed in the hands of an anthropomorphic creature collecting blood from the neck of a captured prisoner.

Based on this iconographic evidence and the presence of the dipper and shield, Alva and Lucho became convinced that the child unearthed earlier was some kind of "assistant" to a royal servant or "attendant" they had just excavated, and that both assistant and attendant served a lord or royal functionary yet to be found in the chamber.

As farfetched as this theory seemed to be, evidence to support it was immediately forthcoming. Beneath a bed of fine silt less than two feet under the attendant, Lucho and Alva cleared the dust from around the now familiar copper straps of what appeared to be another royal coffin.

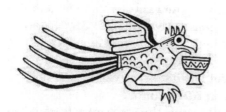

27

Earlier in their excavation, Alva and Lucho had searched for a goblet or royal chalice that Donnan believed should have been buried in the tomb of the lord of the sacrifice ceremony. None had been found. Now, in July and August 1988, as Alva brushed aside the decomposed fragments of the second royal coffin, he knew the reason. There had been no goblet among the burial possessions of the Moche lord because it had been placed in the hands of the High Priest of Sipan.

Alva reached this startling conclusion as he and Lucho removed the last remains of the coffin's planking to reveal an elaborate blanket of lavish gold, silver, and gilded-copper ornaments. Because of the large number of artifacts and their similarity to the burial possessions removed from the previous tomb, Alva and Lucho first believed that they had unearthed the Lord of Sipan's father or son. But this soon had to be ruled out.

Like that of the Lord of Sipan, the tomb of the High Priest contained numerous strings of beads and beaded pectorals that completely covered the shoulders and chest area of the skeleton, each crafted with the same attention to detail, balance, and harmony apparent in the ceramics. But where the occupant of the first tomb had worn ten beads depicting the heads of owls, the occupant of the second had two necklaces of ten beads, each depicting human heads.

Half silver, half gilded gold, each head was about the size and shape of a plum, with eyes of lapis lazuli and teeth of intricately carved shell. Ten of these heads, strung together to form one of the necklaces, revealed smiling, happy faces. The other ten, strung together to form the companion necklace, showed sorrowful, unhappy faces. How the High Priest might have worn the beads, or in what order, Alva could only speculate, but evidence of their use could not be denied, for the holes through which the beads were strung had been enlarged, indicating that the necklaces had been worn regularly and not simply for occasional ritual use.

Atop his head, the High Priest wore a crescent-shaped ornament decorated with matching miniature heads and a pair of gilded-copper ear spools, each as finely crafted as the ornaments excavated from the first tomb, but not as profuse with gold or inlaid with precious stones. Just as it was portrayed in the sacrifice ceremony, the High Priest's headdress ornament hung on a conical helmet, flanked by two strips of sheet metal that had been cut to form a pair of hands reaching out to the heavens.

Beneath the High Priest's nose rested a moon-shaped nose ring; and layer upon layer of bright yellow and red beads were woven into a smock that went down to his knees. As had the Lord of Sipan, the High Priest wore moon-shaped rattles around his waist. Bells in the shape of seashells fringed the bottom of his smock. Dazzling though these ornaments were, the clue that unraveled the mystery of the High Priest's identity lay in his right hand. Instead of a rattle or cutting tool similar to the one Alva had found in the hand of the Lord of Sipan, this skeleton held a goblet or cup identical to the one being presented to the lord in depictions of the sacrifice ceremony.

Made of hammered copper gilded with gold, the goblet was not much larger than a man's cupped hands and may have been intended to contain more than a pint of blood. Decomposition of the metal made it impossible to tell whether it had been used. But judging from the quantity of human and animal remains that accompanied the High Priest in the burial chamber, and the hundred or more ceramics placed in separate niches on all four sides of the burial, the goblet's importance couldn't be overestimated.

To the west of the High Priest's coffin lay two men, aged approximately twenty-five to thirty, placed in separate cane coffins that had also long since decomposed. The man closer to the High Priest lay with his head to the north and his feet to the south, exactly the reverse of the High Priest. His garments, almost totally decomposed, showed that he may have been of high status, something confirmed by the large gilded-copper headdress that had been put on his head at the time of his burial. Beside him, laid out with his head to the south and his feet to the north, rested an almost identical burial. In this case, however, the man had a gilded-copper breast plate, or pectoral, and no headdress. As in the case of the burial of the attendant above and to the right of the High Priest's coffin, Alva viewed both men as royal servants. Placement of their skeletons in neatly proportioned and measured burial chambers and lack of scrambling of the bones indicated that they had died at about the same time, presumably just before or after the High Priest.

In the southwest corner of the burial chamber, at the respective head and feet of the two male skeletons, lay a small rectangular coffin containing a snake, a dog, and a child. Here again, lack of disarticulation of the bones and their careful placement within a specially carved section of the burial chamber indicated that all three had died or been killed at the same time that the High Priest was buried. A simple gilded-copper headdress on the child suggested either a royal birth or some high status. The presence of the dog and the snake, each wrapped in special cotton shrouds, was a further clue to the trio's attachment or association with the High Priest, especially since both animals were represented in depictions of the sacrifice ceremony.

Decomposition of the flesh of both men, the child, and the two animals made it virtually impossible to tell how they died. But this was not the case with the sixth burial, that of a llama unearthed in a cane coffin in the southeast corner of the burial chamber, to the right of the High Priest. An examination of the skeletal remains revealed that the legs of the llama had been tied together, a cut made along the animal's underside, and its insides and head removed. Following what appeared to be

standard Andean tradition, this llama had clearly been a sacrifice, much like the seventh burial, that of a fifteen- to eighteen- year-old girl uncovered to the immediate right of the High Priest, just beneath the attendant.

From the pedestal of clay placed on top of the young girl and the position of the legs of the llama on top of her feet, it was clear that Moche craftsmen had prepared or reserved a place in the tomb for this sacrifice before any of the others. Alva was certain that she had been a sacrifice because of the unusual position her body was in: facedown, right elbow jutted out in front of her, left hand flung behind her. Either she had been ritually killed and flung into the burial chamber or, more likely, she had been pushed inside while still alive, then covered with earth.

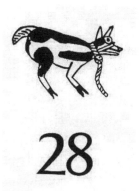

28

Excavation of the tomb of the High Priest continued uninterrupted through the middle of 1989, but none of the human or animal remains unearthed during these nine months would compare in significance to the discovery of a royal Moche burial chamber near La Mina, the site of a long-abandoned gold mine located south of Lambayeque, in the hills above Jequetepeque. Alva learned about the burial chamber on the morning of May 11, 1989, in an unexpected call from an antiquities collector in Trujillo who had become concerned that La Mina might be looted before archaeologists could reach the site.

How the collector learned about the burial chamber was as remarkable as the reason he called an archaeologist and not a tomb looter. But Alva chose not to cross-examine the collector until later. He merely assigned Lucho to take charge at Huaca Rajada and ordered Benedicto to pack food and supplies for an emergency salvage operation in the Jequetepeque Valley. Despite his exhaustion from so many months of continuous excavation, and the many economic and political reasons he had for not stepping between looters and INC officials once again, Alva couldn't miss an opportunity to galvanize support for his campaign to protect Peru's past, especially at another

Moche archaeological site.

According to the collector, who asked that Alva not reveal his name, an unemployed farmer from the small village of Jequetepeque had been plundering graves at nearby Balsar before discovering a promising burial near the rock-strewn entrance to La Mina. As the looter suspected, this burial belonged to an upper-class Inca or Chimu individual, and yielded a few moderately valuable ceramics. After removing these artifacts, however, the looter discovered that Moche clay bricks lined the bottom of the grave. Beneath these bricks the looter unearthed the entrance to a tunnel that had been carved into the hillside, leading to a burial chamber as rich in Moche antiquities as both of the tombs Alva had excavated at Huaca Rajada.

Instead of hiring a team of other huaqueros to help him plunder the site all at once, the original looter used the tomb as a type of savings account, making withdrawals only when he needed cash. Because of the extraordinary high quality of the artifacts reaching the market and the considerable amount of time that elapsed between individual offerings, the Trujillo collector suspected fraud, believing that unscrupulous dealers were manufacturing duplicates of artifacts previously looted from Huaca Rajada. The dubious collector traced the artifacts back to the original looter and identified La Mina as their source. Respect for Alva's handling of the volatile situation at Huaca Rajada had prompted the collector to call him to ask if he could offer La Mina the same protection.

Incredible as the collector's claims sounded, Alva had more than sufficient reason to believe him. Donnan's contacts in Lima and Trujillo had been hearing about a rich Moche tomb in the lower Jequetepeque Valley since the fall of 1988, but had been unable to pinpoint its location. Donnan's contacts had also believed that black-market counterfeiters may have begun reproducing Moche art for the ever-expanding overseas market. Invited to examine and photograph the pieces for the Moche Archive, Donnan determined the gold, silver, and ceramic antiquities to be genuine and of the same approximate vintage as those excavated at Huaca Rajada. Anxious to locate the site, Donnan spent close to a month searching the rim and basin of the valley looking for the telltale backfill that normally results from clandestine plunder. An associate conducted an aerial surveillance in a plane equipped with 35-mm cameras and telephoto lenses. But nothing came of their efforts, and Donnan returned to Los Angeles knowing little more about the site than when he had begun his search. Thanks to the Trujillo collector, Alva now knew why. A single man had discovered the tomb at La Mina, not a team of huaqueros, and he had sought to keep its entrance a closely guarded secret because he hadn't finished looting it.

Alva immediately telephoned police authorities in Trujillo. They recognized Alva's name for the same reasons that the Trujillo collector had: Front-page articles about Alva's saving the fabulous tombs at Huaca Rajada had eclipsed the earlier front-page stories about the Bernal shooting. Alva had become a hero on Peru's north coast. But being a local hero couldn't overcome the severe economic hardships confronting the Trujillo police. Department officials hadn't a single available patrol car in their motor pool to send to the Jequetepeque Valley.

Lucho needed the Bruning's van at Huaca Rajada to transport food, equipment, and artifacts. Alva's other means of transportation was a 1968 Volkswagen Beetle, held together with gaffer's tape. But this had been up on chock blocks since the last El Nino, waiting for Alva to requisition enough money for a new carburetor. Donnan's Chevy truck, however, was parked for safe keeping behind the gated entrance to the Bruning.

Driving south at top speed, Benedicto crossed a

hundred miles of desert before the bleak strips of sand south of Chiclayo became dotted by vegetation and the irrigated green fields leading into the Jequetepeque Valley. Benedicto skirted the edge of these fields, following the wide saucer of the valley until he and Alva came to the small village of Jequetepeque, little more than an open plaza, a cluster of small homes, and a whitewashed mission standing majestically in the center of town. Benedicto didn't slow down until they had passed right through the town, where he took a meandering dirt road up the foothills toward a high, cone-shaped peak.

About a mile from the rock-strewn entrance of La Mina, Benedicto parked the truck to the side of the road. He and Alva then made the rest of the trip on foot, hiking along a path between tall, lichen-encrusted gray rocks. As most tourists to the area knew, the entrance to the mine was on a small plateau, where a few partially excavated trenches and clay-brick structures testified to the former significance of La Mina as a pre- Inca gold mine.

A single looter may have found the entrance to a Moche tomb at La Mina, but others had followed the looter to the site and taken it from him. Alva was certain about this because he saw three huaqueros scurrying from open trenches as he approached, Mauser in hand. Three shots fired over their heads sent them running, leaving Alva to examine the trenches and adjacent burial shaft on his own.

Alva made two immediate observations upon seeing the trenches and adjacent shaft: that the Moche had gone to a considerable amount of trouble to carve a burial chamber out of the rocky shoulder of the hillside, and that looters had damaged the site far more than the Trujillo antiquities collector had imagined.

Leaving Benedicto to stand guard, Alva pointed a flashlight into the narrow opening in the hillside, searched for a foothold, then slowly lowered himself into the shaft.

Unlike the ones at Huaca Rajada, the huaqueros' shaft at La Mina was barely large enough for one man to squeeze his shoulders through, and the cool air inside was still and suffocating. Alva sank inch by inch into the inky blackness until he came to a narrow ledge, where he paused to catch his breath. The familiar bitter aroma from an opened tomb filled his lungs.

Twenty-seven feet beneath the cone-shaped rocks at the shaft's entrance, the huaqueros' tunnel abruptly tripled in size, opening into a ten-by-thirteen-foot rectangular burial chamber that had been dug partly into the bedrock and partly into the earth under the stone peak above. Kneeling in the bottom of the chamber, Alva shone his flashlight into a tomb that had been roofed about seven feet above its clay floor, then sealed with a ton or more of gravel and rock that the huaqueros had not bothered to remove.

Complex geometric designs and colorful pictures of snakes and stingrays were painted on the chamber's interior walls. Akin to the famous murals on a wall at Huaca del Luna, the patterns and colors were clearly of Moche origin and similar in style and iconographic detail to the looted gold and silver objects Donnan had photographed for his Moche Archive at UCLA. Besides these ghostly images, little else remained but fragments of bone, smashed pottery, and small flakes of copper scattered from one end of the room to the other. Any other indication of the identity of the tomb's occupant had long ago vanished or lay concealed in hidden niches.

Months of looking into vacant huaqueros' tunnels had prepared Alva for this eventuality. But it still hurt to see how quickly a handful of looters could plunder a resource as rare as a royal burial chamber. Alva had but one consolation: that in the case of La Mina, a collector had called his attention to a looting in progress, not the police. His attempts to educate the public had begun to bring results: The seeds he had planted at Huaca Rajada had taken root.

Alva also knew from firsthand experience that a looted tomb held secrets that couldn't be obtained from a first or second inspection. Besides the likelihood of finding hidden niches or burial chambers overlooked by huaqueros, an archaeological study of the tomb might reveal more about the mine and buildings adjacent to it as well as something that Andean scholars had long suspected but never been able to prove: that prior to being used as a gold mine, La Mina had been the home of ancient north-coast oracles. A cavern adjacent to the mine had never been adequately mapped or even explored. But for now, however, Alva's chief concern was to set up a salvage operation before huaqueros could inflict any more damage upon the site.

Returning to the shaft that he had followed into the burial chamber, Alva made some mental notes about the layout and architecture of the tomb, then climbed up into the daylight. He and Benedicto covered the entrance as best they could, hiked back to the truck, and drove into the village of Jequetepeque. At the open plaza, Alva approached a group of farmers who had come to sell their produce. His reputation had once again preceded him. Accordingly, it was a simple matter of dipping into excavation funds to hire them to stand guard at La Mina until he could call Donnan at UCLA and arrange for more permanent protection.

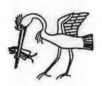

29

La Mina's plundered artifacts received only a lukewarm reception in the previously hot Los Angeles and New York antiquities markets. Not that the merchandise hadn't been top quality. Perhaps it had been of even higher quality than Huaca Rajada's looted antiquities, and more valuable because the tomb had yielded so much less. Hesitation on the part of dealers and collectors came as a result of the March 30, 1988, Customs seizures and pending indictments, which caused the first recorded plunge in the purchase prices of pre-Columbian art in more than a century. Art collectors and antiquities speculators feared that stricter enforcement of existing laws would put them out of business. Advocates of Peru's cultural patrimony hoped that the highly publicized cases would be the turning point in their effort to preserve their country's past, and would force the return of artifacts in private and public collections in the United States. More significant in the long run, Peru's legal claim of blanket ownership of all Peruvian pre-Columbian antiquities raised a legal question about any nation's right to declare blanket ownership of its cultural heritage. If Peru could win in United States courts, then so could Mexico, Ecuador, Bolivia, and a host of other sources of pre-Columbian art.

Jamaican-born Spurgeon Smith, the thirty-one-year-old attorney chosen to prosecute the case, had little or no prior experience in the field of pre-Columbian antiquities or art smuggling. A graduate of Howard University in Washington, D.C., Smith had worked in firms in New York and Los Angeles before joining United States Attorney Robert Bonner's major crimes unit in 1988. Smith, assigned the antiquities case in June of that same year, suddenly found himself pitted against some of the highest paid and most influential specialists in the country.

John Henry Merryman, Stanford University's expert on international art law, and Edward L. Wolf, an attorney with Arnold & Porter in Washington, D.C., representing the American Association of Dealers in Ancient, Oriental, and Primitive Art, spearheaded the crack legal team, generating a torrent of litigation that brought the judicial process to a virtual standstill. Embroiled in what prosecutors described as a "deluge" of pretrial motions and expert analysis work, United States Attorney Smith declined to hand down any indictments until November 17, 1988, more than a year after Michael Kelly met Gaston Wallace on the ocean promenade in Ventura.

Besides the time-consuming task of categorizing and labeling the 1,391 art objects Customs agents seized, Smith had to process almost two dozen requests for suppression of evidence not specifically mentioned in the search warrants, including art that was not deemed to be pre-Columbian and documents that were not specifically part of the criminal investigation. Under Rule 41 of the criminal code, law enforcers also had to return firearms, illegal narcotics, and pornography seized in the course of their searches. Public disclosure of items not specifically mentioned in the search warrants became a hotly contested issue, especially in the case of a marital dispute arising over alleged "sex tapes" produced by one of David Swetnam's clients without the knowledge or consent of participants.

Another hotly contested issue concerned who would pay the sizable bills for the storage of artifacts at Cookes Crating. Bills for the eight-month period leading up to the indictments amounted to more than twelve thousand dollars, and could conceivably become tens of thousands of dollars if litigants contested ownership or failed to forfeit seized artifacts. Of the thirteen or more individuals involved in the seizures, only two, Charles Craig, the retired banker from Santa Barbara, and Murray Gell-Mann, the physicist from Pasadena, willingly chose to forfeit their property to Peru. By agreement, Craig turned over forty-five artifacts, and Gell-Mann, twenty-three, the rest of their collections deemed to have been from other countries.

Early on in the pretrial phase of litigation, Ronald Nessim and Edward Wolf, co-counsel for Ben Johnson, argued for the return of Johnson's entire pre-Columbian collection. Defense contended that seizure of the 330 artifacts and the documentation that accompanied them put an unfair financial and physical hardship on their client's ability to buy, sell, and restore antiquities. Unless the government could make a strong case for their seizures and, in the process, prematurely tip their hand to the identity of undercover informant S-3 OX, the artifacts had to be returned to Johnson.

Attorney Patrick Hallinan, counsel for Jacquelyn and David Swetnam, made a similar request, claiming that the five hundred or more items taken from his clients represented their entire livelihood. Hallinan also communicated outrage at having his clients' home surrounded by armed Customs agents, acting, in one of his client's words, "as if it were a raid on a crack-house."

Ben Johnson was sitting in his wheelchair in the United

States Customs office in Oxnard when he first connected Michael Kelly to the government seizures and impending indictments. His realization that Kelly was a spy caused Johnson's hands to start shaking and his blood pressure to rise dramatically. Blood vessels burst in one of his eyes and paramedics had to be called to take him to the hospital.

Fearing reprisal from Miguel Berckemeyer, Michael Kelly demanded to be put in the Witness Protection Program, a request that sat on United States Attorney Robert Bonner's desk for over three months before being denied. Kelly didn't understand Bonner's decision until the middle of November 1989, when prosecutors finally handed down their indictment and revealed the limited scope of the case against Kelly's former associates.

Either United States attorneys became intimidated by the army of lawyers arrayed against them, or they believed that justice would best be served by limiting the indictment to just two individuals, Jacquelyn and David Swetnam, charged with ten counts of conspiracy, smuggling, and related customs violations. Of these ten counts, each calling for a maximum penalty of five years in prison and a fine of $250,000, all were based on only twenty individual artifacts smuggled into the United States by Michael Kelly in one of the three shipments.

Prosecutors had decided to overlook the remaining 1,369 seized artifacts and to ignore completely Miguel Berckemeyer, Fred Drew, Ben Johnson, and the twenty or more dealers, collectors, and middlemen involved in the smuggling operation. By limiting the indictment in this way, the attorneys also avoided the thorny legal question of whether the seized artifacts were the stolen property of Peru or rightfully belonged to United States collectors.

United States v. Swetnam would never reach trial. In return for the government's dropping charges against

Jacquelyn, David pleaded guilty on May 12, 1989, to a four-count indictment, later changed to three counts of receiving and causing the importation of nine smuggled artifacts. Taking full advantage of the reduced charges, Patrick Hallinan argued to the court that his client could have legally imported the antiquities into the United States from England but chose to declare them "personal effects" to avoid "confusion" among United States Customs agents. The vast majority of seized documents, meticulously collected and prepared by Gaston Wallace, were never introduced as evidence. Nor was Michael Kelly ever brought to the witness stand to testify.

Judge Richard Gadbois, clearly unimpressed by the evidence as presented, had reservations about sentencing Swetnam to any jail time. But the judge concluded that a clear-cut violation of customs laws required that Swetnam receive a prison term, and sentenced him on June 26, 1989, to six months at the federal minimum-security prison camp at Boron, California, earning Swetnam the dubious distinction of being the first person in United States history to serve time for smuggling Peruvian artifacts into the United States.

Upon Swetnam's release after serving only four months of his sentence, all but 8 of the original 362 artifacts seized from him were returned. Among the 354 was the most valuable artifact of all: the golden jaguar head. In an ironic twist, David Swetnam eventually lost possession of this antiquity, for it was claimed by Patrick Hallinan in lieu of outstanding legal fees.

Enraged by the United States government's feeble attempt to prosecute the smugglers, advocates of Peru's cultural patrimony named Ben Johnson and six others in a separate civil lawsuit, citing Peru's 1929 ownership laws pertaining to pre- Columbian antiquities and a 1981 executive agreement committing the United States to assisting Peru in recovering stolen cultural property. Archaeologists in both countries hailed the move as an important step forward and chided United States Attorney Robert Bonner in the criminal case for bowing to political pressures brought on by the antiquities lobby.

Before the civil suit could move forward, however, United States attorneys caught Peruvian officials off guard by declaring that the 1981 agreement signed by Ronald Reagan didn't provide for legal aid or advice from attorneys or government agents. Thus, in the critical opening rounds of the civil suit, Peru couldn't turn to Customs agents for help in sifting through the mountains of documentary evidence seized during the raid. Peru also found itself liable for hundreds of thousands of dollars in potential court fees, legal services, and storage costs. Worse still, the prosecution didn't have a lawyer in Los Angeles prepared to argue a complex test case in international law with the formidable likes of Edward Wolf and the American Association of Dealers in Ancient, Oriental, and Primitive Art.

George Roberts, a Los Angeles physicist and one of Peru's most avid and active allies, offered to steer the case through the criminal justice system at his own expense. Since Roberts was not an attorney, he recruited Noel Keyes, a retired Pepperdine University law professor, at that moment recovering from triple bypass surgery in Corona Del Mar, California. Keyes agreed to represent Peru on the condition that Roberts obtain an experienced litigator as co-counsel. Meryl Macklin, an associate at the prestigious Los Angeles legal firm of Heller, Ehrman, White & McAuliffe, agreed to step in on a pro bono basis.

After reviewing the case, however, Macklin and Roberts were soon at odds over how best to proceed.

Macklin sought to make an accommodation by accepting a settlement from Johnson and the co-conspirators named in the suit, a step, she maintained, that would ensure the repatriation of a large number of antiquities to Peru and provide income to cover storage and legal fees. Moreover, she believed that the facts of the case didn't warrant making Peru v. Johnson a test case at all.

Roberts rejected any settlement outright, provoking Macklin to withdraw less than one month before the trial was scheduled to begin. Because of Ben Johnson's declining health, requests for a postponement were denied. By default, Noel Keyes, who had virtually no trial experience, became Peru's sole attorney.

As representatives on both sides of the case knew, success or failure of Peru v. Johnson turned on the distinction between illegal exports and theft. In other words, Peru couldn't bring suit against United States citizens under its own export laws because the United States was not obligated to enforce these laws. But the United States was obligated to enforce laws regarding stolen property, as it did in a landmark 1977 criminal case, United States v. McClain, in which antiquities dealer Patty McClain was found guilty of violating the National Stolen Property Act for importing Mexican pre-Columbian artifacts without obtaining export permits.

Establishing that Johnson's pre-Columbian collection consisted of stolen goods was harder to support than in the criminal case against McClain because Johnson did not directly participate in smuggling the antiquities out of the country. He had only purchased them once they had arrived. Peru also had to establish that the artifacts came from the sites in Peru that the plaintiffs alleged.

John Merryman, who appeared in behalf of Johnson, testified that Peru had never before enforced its law of blanket ownership and did so now only because foreigners had purchased the antiquities. Like Alan Sawyer, a renowned pre-Columbian art expert who also testified on Johnson's behalf, Merryman cited the poor record that the INC had in enforcing its laws. The official INC antiquities registry was designed as the guardian of cultural assets, but it was notoriously disorganized, and the institute itself was scorned for doing little to prevent the looting of its archaeological sites. Peru also had 251 laws and rules affecting pre-Columbian artifacts, many of which contradicted one another.

Noel Keyes was clearly unprepared for the high-powered witnesses who rose to Johnson's defense. He also had trouble obtaining a subpoena for the comprehensive mountain of photographs, documents, canceled checks, and address books that linked Johnson to the other co-conspirators. As a result, all Keyes offered in evidence was the testimony of Michael Kelly, who freely admitted that he hadn't personally sold stolen pre- Columbian objects to Johnson but had merely been present when Johnson had negotiated to purchase them from Swetnam.

Instead of offering the expertise of Alva, who had already examined and identified photographs of the pieces seized from Johnson's collection, Peru enlisted Francisco Iriarte, the same archaeologist who claimed to have made the original discoveries at Huaca Rajada and who later tried to engineer Alva's downfall. On the witness stand, Iriarte was unable to differentiate between Moche and Chimu artistic styles or identify any objects that may have come from Huaca Rajada.

In the end, United States District Judge William P. Gray ruled in favor of Johnson, citing the prosecution's failure to prove to his satisfaction that any of the pre-Columbian pieces in Johnson's collection had come from Peru, or that they were exported after 1929, when Peru's ownership laws took effect. Gray also held that Kelly's testimony regarding the objects was hearsay, and that Peru's claim of ownership based on the statements made by Iriarte and others was uncertain because similar artifacts had been found in archaeological sites in Bolivia and Ecuador.

"It all came down to money," George Roberts said, expressing his despair that a poor country such as Peru could not effectively challenge the art and antiquities lobby in the United States courts. "They won and we lost."

PART 6

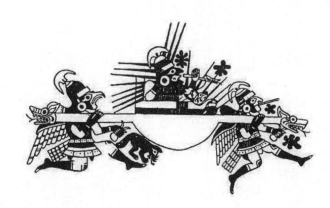

OLD LORD OF SIPAN

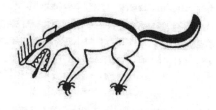

30

Amid highly controversial allegations of mismanagement and a conflict of interest, physicist George Roberts abandoned his representation of the government of Peru, leaving behind a mass of unpaid bills, bitter resentments between Customs agents and prosecutors, and a resounding defeat for advocates of Peru's cultural patrimony. But allegations aimed at Roberts in late 1989 and early 1990 were tame by comparison to those leveled at Donnan and Alva.

In a stinging indictment published in *Art and Antiques* magazine in May 1990, PBS television journalist Carl Nagin called Donnan an "advance man" for smugglers because of his practice of photographing looted artifacts and for not coming to the aid of Peru during its highly publicized court cases. Donnan initially ignored Nagin's commentary, but when the same remarks cropped up a second time in an article by Brian Alexander in *Science* magazine in November 1990, Donnan responded in a matter-of-fact letter to the editor, stating his case in print much as he expressed himself to colleagues at UCLA: that he had never made a secret of his practice of photographing artifacts held in private and public collections, and that his sole motive in doing so was to preserve information that might otherwise be lost.

Museums and funding agencies took his side in the matter, absolving Donnan of any fault. Privately, however, many of the professor's supporters voiced concern. Like others in the scientific community, they chose to view the criticisms of Donnan as less an attack on one man than a reflection of the growing change in the standards and practices of collectors and archaeologists. No place was this change seen more clearly than in President George Bush's request in June 1989 for the United States Information Agency to review all current United States policy governing the importation and sale of pre-Columbian artifacts.

At the same time that Nagin attacked Donnan in print, Enrique Limo, a Peruvian politician seeking reelection in Chiclayo, launched a much-publicized investigative probe of Alva. Based on allegations from an anonymous source, Limo claimed that Alva had committed fraud by embezzling INC funds and falsifying excavation records in order to steal artifacts from Huaca Rajada.

During what Alva called the darkest hour in his career, a team of police and INC officials arrived at the Bruning and seized excavation diaries, financial records, and inventories. Limo scheduled a televised press conference anticipating a guilty verdict. But to his embarrassment, investigators concluded that not only had Alva kept track of the collections under his supervision but he had increased the museum's holdings by pouring much of his own salary into its endeavors. Alva's excavation at Huaca Rajada had prospered, but Alva himself had not.

All charges were summarily dismissed. However, in the process of helping police and INC officials sort through museum records, Alva uncovered a discrepancy that Limo had neglected to find. A pair of small gold ornaments had indeed been taken from the Huaca Rajada collection. Investigators hadn't realized that they were missing because Marcial Montessa had never logged them as having been found. Alva hadn't noticed the oversight because he had been too preoccupied in packing soil samples and artifacts for shipment to the University of Mainz for restoration and analysis.

Under the assumption that Montessa had merely made a clerical error or that the artifacts had accidently been misplaced, Alva decided not to call attention to the two missing ornaments. Instead, he and a Lima colleague initiated an investigation of their own, resulting in an unpleasant discovery: that two similar ornaments in Montessa's care had been sold on the Lima antiquities market in January 1990. Coincidentally, Montessa had earned enough money in the last two months of 1989 to purchase a small house outside Chiclayo. Unable to account for his newfound prosperity or to produce the two gold ornaments, Montessa quietly resigned.

Unfortunately for both Alva and Donnan, the fanfare that resulted from Nagin's article, Limo's allegations of mismanagement, and Montessa's departure stole much of the thunder from the truly extraordinary discoveries that had been made at La Mina and Huaca Rajada in the months immediately after the excavation of the High Priest's tomb. Donnan himself, overwhelmed by the sheer amount of artifacts, pronounced Huaca Rajada to be the richest archaeological site ever excavated in the Americas. He compared the discoveries made at the site, and those made at La Mina, to "finding a bible" for a culture previously believed to have had none.

Donnan had not exaggerated. Alfredo Narvaez, an archaeologist from the University of Trujillo, on a grant administered by Donnan and funded by UCLA, had begun his salvage operation of La Mina the same month that Alva had first visited the site. His research resulted in the publication of many fascinating observations about the tomb and the cave nearby: Like Huaca Rajada, La Mina had been a sacred site long before and long after a royal Moche burial had been placed there; and just as Huaca Rajada may have served as the ceremonial headquarters for the administrative capital at Pampa Grande, La Mina and nearby Balsar may have served as a headquarters for Pacatnamu.

Narvaez's excavation also resulted in the discovery of sixteen magnificent ceramics that Moche craftsmen had sealed into hidden niches carved into the earth on either side of the tomb entrance. Four of the ceramics were sculpted to depict seated persons, perhaps politicians or clan leaders. Others represented owls and felines. And all were nearly identical in design to the gold, silver, and gilded-copper ornaments known to have been plundered from the tomb.

Donnan, who examined and photographed the looted objects in the homes of collectors and dealers, concluded that these antiquities were also identical to artifacts that had been plundered nearly thirty years earlier at Loma Negra, a site located in the far north, in the valley of Piura, and were now on permanent display at the Metropolitan Museum of Art in New York. These treasures also resembled antiquities in Enrico Poli's collection, unearthed in the late 1970s at Balsar, less than a mile south of La Mina.

Using the burials at Huaca Rajada as a textbook model, archaeologists realized that all of these artifacts were the personal property of numerous Moche lords presiding over separate, perhaps mutually hostile valley kingdoms. Donnan and Alva had no way of knowing how much contact these rulers may have had with each other, but the existence of similar findings in tombs hundreds of miles from one another attested to a shared concept of kingship, civic responsibility, and religious belief. In other words, the valley kingdoms of the Moche operated much like the royal houses of medieval Europe.

Knowledge gained from the two burials at Huaca Rajada and the looted objects from La Mina also provided Alva a greater appreciation of the rich ceremonial life that lords of Peru's valley kingdoms presided over. The importance of the sacrifice ceremony had been apparent since Alva's excavation had begun. But only now, when he could excavate without fear of marauding huaqueros, and with his family joining him for a long overdue reunion, did Huaca Rajada reveal macabre proof to Alva that the Moche confined ritual violence to the controlled environment high atop their pyramids.

An eerie clue appeared in late June and early July 1989, when Lucho opened the largest cut to have been found in the pyramid, a rectangle more than sixty feet long and forty-five feet wide on the southernmost portion of the platform. Eight to ten feet beneath this cut, under a literal mountain of clay-brick fill and small stones, Alva uncovered nine other cuts, leading to six individual chambers.

Each of the six chambers, measuring approximately seven feet square and six feet deep, had been carved into the platform at about A.D. 300, the same time or slightly later than the two royal tombs Alva and Lucho had previously excavated. None of these chambers, however, could be considered tombs in the same sense as the two previous burial chambers. Although each contained large numbers of colorful ceramics, gold, silver, and gilded-copper ornaments, and other symbols of Moche power and might, no complete human burials were found inside.

Human and animal remains placed in these chambers consisted of large collections of various body parts, such as arms and legs, fingers and toes—not complete corpses.

Much like the cache of ceramics associated with the first tomb, the three hundred to four hundred pots removed from the six individual chambers had been mass-produced in molds conforming to one of three basic designs: that of an open, pear-shaped beaker or vase about six inches high and four inches wide, with the head of a warrior incised on the top and hands clasped around its sides; a similar beaker, but smaller, about four inches high and two inches wide; and, finally, crudely produced miniature clay figurines of warriors and politicians about four inches high and two inches wide.

Distributed among the groupings often to fifteen pots were gold, silver, and gilded-copper ornaments depicting shields, armor, and weapons wrapped together with golden thread, all in the same miniature proportions as the clay figurines. Alva instantly recognized the parcels as tiny "weapons bundles," the tribute that warriors presented to the Moche lord at the start of the sacrifice ceremony. Moche iconography offered numerous examples of these weapons bundles, but none had ever been excavated archaeologically.

Alva had no doubt that each of the weapons bundles represented one or more actual sacrifices, for just underneath lay the collections of scattered human body parts apparently hacked off with a sharpened blade. In one chamber Alva counted more than six feet, three hands, and an assortment of other bones. Another contained a pair of human heads, eyeing one another from across opposite ends of the chamber.

At first, Alva believed that these gruesome reminders of the sacrifice ceremony had been placed inside the platform as an offering to another lord or High Priest buried nearby.

Evidence to support this conclusion came with the excavation of a nine-by-fourteen-foot cut located thirty feet west of the tomb of the High Priest, in the general vicinity of the sacrificial chambers. But this cut, excavators soon discovered, led to a shaft that had apparently been abandoned before a royal burial or sacrificial chamber had been placed inside.

A closer inspection of the inside floor revealed something Alva and Lucho had not previously encountered: evidence of a second cut underneath the first. Based on carbon 14 tests taken at various levels of the pyramid, and the architectural examination of the various building phases, Alva reached the logical conclusion that Moche engineers had either forgotten about a previous burial made in the platform or miscalculated and begun to carve a chamber into a section of the pyramid that already contained one.

Eager to test his hypothesis, Alva ordered Lucho to remove the fill carefully from inside the abandoned cut, then carve a two-by-two-foot hole into the bottom to look for decomposed roof timbers, copper straps, or the planks on a coffin. To their surprise, none of these things were found. Instead, more than thirty-six feet beneath the top of the pyramid platform and twenty-one feet deeper than the first two tombs, Lucho exposed the remains of the upper portion of a cotton shroud.

Excavation elsewhere on the platform stopped completely as Alva lit a lantern and lowered himself into the hole. Probing carefully beneath the rotted fragments of the shroud, Alva dusted a three-by-four-inch rectangle clear of loose fill and decomposed cotton fibers. Beneath his brush, in a hollow about the size of his fist, lay the first of ten solid-gold spiders, poised on a spiraling web spun from thin gold threads around the neck of a man buried more than three hundred years earlier than the Lord of

Sipan or the High Priest.

Nacho, Alva's twelve-year-old son, would name the occupant of the third tomb "Senor Arana," or "Spiderman." Alva merely called him "El Viejo Senor de Sipan," or the "Old Lord of Sipan."

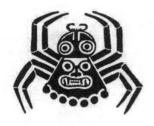

31

If the two previous tombs had provided Alva and Donnan a textbook model for royal Moche burials, excavation of the third tomb gave archaeologists an unparalleled opportunity to see how burial practices had changed over the course of three centuries. Just as the platform itself had grown larger and more elaborate, so too had the burials placed inside.

Alva first glimpsed the more modest, unadorned nature of the third tomb on August 4, 1989, after excavators had removed the mountain of bricks from around its perimeter. Unlike the two previous tombs, this one lacked the large, rectangular, beamed chamber and planked coffin that Alva had come to expect. No human or animal remains accompanied the lone interment, no hidden niches had been carved into the chamber walls, and no guardian was placed above it.

From a technical point of view, absence of multiple coffins and a complicated arrangement of burials made this tomb all the easier to excavate. But this didn't mean that its contents were any less spectacular or rich in precious metals. Burial goods from this tomb had a leaner, bolder style, evoking a vital and energetic period in Moche culture. Alva could not be certain, but the artifacts suggested that the lord played a more active role in the society that he presided over. Lords may even have assumed the responsibilities later accorded high priests.

Alva's examination of the tomb's architecture revealed burial practices similar to contemporary north-coast customs. Moche laborers had carved an eight-foot shaft straight down into the platform, creating a rectangular chamber that measured six and a half feet long and three and a half feet wide. Into this chamber were placed human remains and burial possessions wrapped in a cotton shroud and then bundled in a cane mat. Because of the narrow confines of the shaft, Alva concluded that the cane bundle had been lowered into the chamber by ropes held from above.

Around the cane-wrapped remains were twenty-six ceramic jars, painted in the typical Moche style of red on white slip. As a group, they were quite distinctive from the ceramics Alva had previously found. They were about a foot and a half high and ten inches wide, about twice the size of the others, and had many brightly painted designs upon them, similar to patterns that appeared on Moche shields. Although the contents of the ceramic pots had long ago evaporated or decomposed, discoloration on the clay inside attested to the fact that they had been filled with offerings of food and drink.

Along one side of the body were weapons that clearly had been used to hunt animals or other game. These included gold and silver knives, copper spear points, and gilded war clubs, all possessions that lent power and authority to the lord's life. Many of the weapons had been systematically broken and crushed before being placed in the grave, a means, Alva theorized, of enabling the lord to take them into the afterlife, or of preventing anyone except the lord from using them after his death.

Beneath the ten magnificent spider beads, each molded to portray a human face on its back, Alva uncovered a funerary mask that had slipped off the fragmented skull. As with five other masks found in the burial chamber, one eye socket was made of hammered gold and the other was left vacant, perhaps so the lord could keep one eye on this world and one on the afterlife.

As in the case of the two previous royal burials, numerous fan-shaped rattles had been tied around his waist. Each of the hollow spheres contained small copper balls on their circumference, perhaps for producing sound when shaken during the course of the ceremonies that the lord presided over. Palm-sized cutting blades, unearthed nearby, suggested that these rattles may have been the precursor to the type found in tomb one, in which rattle and cutting blade were combined into a single unit.

Remains of several textiles partly covered the lower half of the skeletal remains. Like the Moche textiles from other sites, these had been damaged by moisture from devastating El Nino rains. But because of the great depth of this tomb inside the pyramid, the textiles showed less damage than those from the two previous tombs. Partial remains of seven distinct textiles were found, including three tapestries with complex iconography depicting the Fanged Deity in his temple, or perched on a throne, holding a severed head in one hand, a knife in the other.

Under the funerary mask were a solid-gold nose ring and two ear ornaments. Below these ornaments stretched the arc of a solid-gold back flap, moon-shaped masks displaying the heads of bats and cats with giant shell teeth, and strings of necklaces. A pectoral of shells, beads, and lapis lazuli was draped over the remains of the chest cavity, alongside vast quantities of other miniature metal, shell, and stone ornaments.

Excitement grew when Lucho's brush revealed a find as spectacular as anything previously excavated: a miniature figure holding a gold war club and shield, much like the one found on the ear spool of the first tomb, but this one was part of an elaborate nose ring on a tarnished silver plate. Alva and Lucho marveled when this piece came to light. Atop his head, the figure wore a headdress of thinly hammered gold with an owl in the center. His turquoise eyes had pupils of black stone and his nose ornament actually moved to the touch. In terms of craftsmanship and delicacy of execution, this was without doubt the most beautiful nose ornament ever found, and it certainly ranked as one of the finest objects produced by the Moche.

However, the object that would capture Alva's greatest attention was a gilded-copper figurine unlike anything he had ever before found. With the head and legs of a human and the claws of a crab, the gilded-copper idol was more than two feet tall: unprecedented for Moche figurines. Later restoration showed that the strange creature had once been mounted on a fabric banner covered with hundreds of gilded metal plates about the size of coins. Alva and his men immediately called the crab "Ulluchu Man" because the banner yielded the first samples of this ancient Peruvian fruit yet discovered.

As Alva knew, the ulluchu was part of the papaya family. Laden with symbolism, it could be seen on numerous Moche ceramics that showed scenes relating to ritualistic warfare and the drinking of a prisoner's blood. A prominent theory held by Alva and other Andean scholars suggested that the ulluchu had anticoagulant properties that were useful in preventing clotting before a human or animal's blood was consumed.

Discovery of ulluchu fruit seemed only natural, given the symbolism of the creatures depicted on the ornaments unearthed in each of the three tombs. Bats, owls, spiders, crabs, and snakes were all creatures who ate their victims, in some cases feasting off their victim's blood for a period of hours or even days, just as the Moche lord fulfilled his sacred obligation at the sacrifice ceremony by consuming the blood of prisoners.

The intertwining of art with violence was no longer a mystery, for the ceremonies themselves called Moche art into existence, and may have been the reason why the Moche survived for nearly a thousand years while neighboring cultures vanished without trace. Mastering the "art" of ritual violence and confining it to the controlled environment high atop their pyramids, the Moche, like the Maya, may have succeeded in preventing eruptions of internal strife in their communities at large.

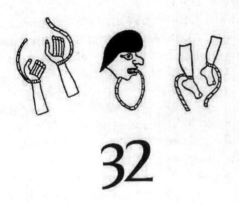

32

In the months ahead, Alva had little time to ponder the significance of Ulluchu Man or the trove of two thousand or more artifacts that Huaca Rajada yielded. Nor was Alva, as a trained field archaeologist, suited for scholarly tasks of this nature. But despite the intensity of his activities, he still made it a point to lecture schoolchildren and others about his findings, and to hike each evening up the side of the neighboring pyramid, as he had on the morning Ernil Bernal had been shot. Alva found the commanding height expressly suited to tackle the one question that had perplexed him since his childhood: Why had a civilization as sophisticated and powerful as the Moche vanished so quickly from the north coast? The artifacts that he and Lucho had unearthed in the three years of excavation provided important clues.

Alva could now prove that tremendous wealth was concentrated in the hands of a few individuals who lived in great opulence and were surrounded by nobility. Donnan's research at looted sites such as La Mina, Balsar, and Loma Negra indicated that every valley had one or more royal courts. As the culture evolved, royalty in the individual valley kingdoms may have had less and less contact with the common people, yet were connected to one another, perhaps through intermarriage or common beliefs. And just as European royalty shared a concept of what constituted the trappings of wealth and power, such as crowns, scepters, thrones, servants, and imperial carriages, the Moche royalty shared similar insignia of status: massive moon- shaped gold and silver headdresses, nose and ear ornaments, rattles, beaded pectorals, and litters.

However, unlike European royalty, who passed on their trappings to successive generations, the Moche took their treasures to the grave. Custom demanded that these treasures be replaced for the new lord by artisans and the legions of miners and metallurgists who supported them. This perpetual demand for luxury items led to the rise and formation of craft guilds, the single most important factor in nurturing the arts and technology so characteristic of the Moche culture.

But these same factors must also have sapped the energies of Moche society by placing an unparalleled burden on its population. Nowhere would this have been more true than at Pampa Grande, the archaeological site that Alva believed was the administrative headquarters and home for the Moche in the Lambayeque Valley. As many as ten thousand people may have lived in clusters of rooms there: retainers and servants to the royal court, laborers who built the grand temples and pyramids, and artisans whose wares bore the signature of Moche genius. However, around A.D. 550, the structures of the rich and powerful ruling class appear to have been burned and plundered, after which Pampa Grande was abandoned and Chimu and other pre-Inca cultures moved in to take the place of the Moche in the valley. The intrusive burials in the northernmost section of Huaca Rajada indicated that the invading people may not have even realized that Moche royalty had been buried there. All they may have known about Huaca Rajada was its significance as the Moche "House of the Moon."

Perhaps, Alva theorized, a peasant revolution caused the demise of the Moche culture. Later catastrophes such as the documented flood from an El Nino in A.D. 750 or invasions of Huari tribes from the south around the same time may have provided the final crushing blow. Huaca Rajada wouldn't provide the final proof for such a theory because the most recent level of the pyramid had been completed in the year 300, and the Moche had survived for at least another four hundred years.

Hiking the serpentine trail to the top of Huaca Rajada on the blistering hot morning of November 10, 1989, tailed by local villagers and a group of students from the University of Trujillo, Alva was rightly hopeful about the impact his excavation would have on future scholarship. At no time in modern history had the royal class of an Andean culture as old as the Moche come into such sharp focus. Nor had scholars ever obtained such startling evidence of the Moche's superior technical skills and mastery of craft: greater than the Maya, the Aztec, or the Inca. More important to Alva, however, his excavation had become a rallying point in a campaign to protect his nation's past, a contemporary asset as valuable to Peru as Machu Picchu had been a century earlier.

Alva had but one regret. In order to continue excavating, he and his men had to dismantle Huaca Rajada brick by brick until there was nothing left. By the year 2000 the pyramid that had stood for more than a millennium would exist only in photographs and in the minds of the men who had taken it apart.

But Alva had no intention of letting such a melancholy thought spoil his morning, for Max and Domingo had cleared the fill from a cut in the southern corner of the platform to reveal another burial, clearly a guardian for yet another royal tomb. And at the same time that Alva and Lucho planned to begin excavating that tomb, a 747 was set to leave Los Angeles International Airport carrying the first shipment of plundered artifacts that United States collectors had ever returned to a Peruvian archaeological site.

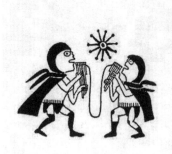

33

Don Enrico Poli, the proud possessor of the largest privately held collection of Huaca Rajada gold, was not invited by the INC to attend the December 2, 1989, ceremony held at the Lima airport to commemorate the formal return to Peru of the 123 artifacts forfeited by United States collectors and dealers. For reasons that seemed clear to everyone but Poli, INC officials also did not invite him to the more formal event held in the newly opened Museo de la Nacion on December 7, in which President Alan Garcia honored physicist Murray Gell-Mann. Like retired United States diplomat Fred Drew, at that moment hiding from police at the home of his son, Poli had been left off all official invitation lists.

Poli himself rejected any notion of ever being arrested, as he dismissed rumors that his telephone was tapped or his mail opened before being delivered. To an undercover investigator from the United States Information Agency posing as an amateur archaeologist and rich patron of the arts, Poli denied violating any Peruvian laws in his quest to build the ultimate pre-Columbian art collection.

"It is I, not Alva, who should receive an award," Poli told the USIA investigator. "If it weren't for me the rest of the artifacts would be in London, or Munich, or Tokyo. I alone am responsible for keeping the treasures of Huaca Rajada in Peru."

To this investigator, as to others he invited on fifty-dollar tours of his collection, Poli talked of the risks he had taken to acquire the artifacts, romanticizing the intrigue that had cost one man his life and sent at least four others to prisons in the United States and Peru. Believing that he had succeeded where others had failed gave Poli great pleasure. He alone, so he claimed, had amassed the "lion's share" of Huaca Rajada's treasures.

Poli met his visitor in front of a two-inch steel gate on Lord Cochran Avenue and invited him to sit for a few minutes in his heavily decorated living room and study. Leaning back in an overstuffed leather armchair, framed in a halo of gold and silver crucifixes hanging from the ceiling, he told the investigator about the morning his contacts related the harrowing story of how Ernil Bernal had become trapped in his tunnel at Huaca Rajada. Poli boasted about the time he had run through the streets of Trujillo with suitcases of cash and how he had conducted business directly with the Bernals. Besides photographs of artifacts he had been invited to buy, Poli offered into evidence a ledger that he used to keep track of his important purchases.

Removing the ledger from a sixteenth-century cabinet against the wall, Poli laid it open on his lap and began rattling off purchase prices and dates. He paused only once: to gloat over the travails of a fellow collector from whom he had made his most recent purchases. Unlike others listed in Poli's ledger, this collector, a known cocaine producer, bought looted Huaca Rajada gold as a hedge against narcotics seizures. Each time police confiscated a major shipment of cocaine, Poli's contact had to sell another artifact. A rash of recent seizures had increased Poli's holdings by one third.

Impatient to see his collection, Poli's visitor asked about the gold rattle, believed by the police to have been the last looted artifact to have been sold by Ernil Bernal before his death. Poli smiled, raised a bony finger on one of his long and expressive hands, and pointed to his two private galleries in the courtyard outside, the next stop on the grand tour.

He declined to comment on his elaborate security system as he led the investigator into the courtyard and through the entrance to the first gallery, a building not much larger than a guest house. But it was clear from the vault-like entrance, the reinforced concrete walls, the metal bars over the air vents, and the infrared cameras that little short of an armed invasion could penetrate his "holy of holies," as he referred to his collection.

Inside, the investigator faced a massive seventeenth-century altarpiece encrusted with gold-leaf and polychrome carvings of angels and archangels. Lit candles, placed on the altar, cast a heavenly light across a staggering assemblage of some six hundred carvings, paintings, and other religious treasures that had once embellished small parishes and missions high in the Andes. Except for a brief reference he made about a greedy priest, Poli declined to explain how he had obtained them.

Poli steered his visitor past more gold and silver treasures to a room devoted exclusively to the masterpieces of pre-Columbian Peru. Recessed lighting illuminated shelves containing Chavin ceramics, Nazca textiles, Moche stirrup-spouts, Chimu bottles, Huari statues, and ritual carvings that once decorated Inca temples.

Young Alva would have been at home in this

collection, for Poli had a long-standing policy that his visitors could handle the ceramics, in order to "commune with the ancients" or "feel their spiritual energy." Poli argued that contemporary art lacked spiritual energy because society had "emasculated" its artists by turning their work into more decoration. "Art has lost its purpose," he proclaimed.

Up to this point the tour was merely a prelude to the main attraction: an alcove devoted exclusively to looted Moche and Chimu gold and silver artifacts located in the adjacent building. Poli kept the light turned off in this building until he had led the investigator into the special alcove. "It's for dramatic effect," Poli announced, suddenly flooding the room with spotlights.

Dramatic presentations were hardly necessary, for the artifacts themselves shone with a brilliance that no trick of light could have heightened. Gold and silver pectorals, back flaps, ear spools, tumi knives, rattles, and figurines were displayed in cases on the floor. Moche headdresses from Balsar and necklaces from La Mina glistened on the walls.

Poli ushered his visitor to the corner that contained his Huaca Rajada collection. As he had for other special guests, among them foreign diplomats and influential businessmen, Poli volunteered to model the antiquities, calling himself the real "Lord of Sipan."

Dressed in more than fifteen pounds of looted gold and silver, Poli appeared less a mystic than an aging Midas. His "theories" about the Moche, all cribbed from articles about Huaca Rajada, were impressive only to someone who hadn't heard lectures by Alva or Donnan. As knowledgeable as Poli claimed to be, he hadn't yet realized that Ernil and his men had plundered more than one tomb, or that the large "death masks" he had on display were actually giant beads from the necklace of a high priest.

Asked about the eventual disposition of his collection, Poli guardedly talked about a wing in one of the national museums that would someday have his name on it, a project that hadn't gone beyond the planning stages since he first had begun to discuss making a bequest to the government of Peru more than ten years earlier. A far higher priority appeared to be Poli's need to have his vast art collection registered, and hence protected, under current law.

In this regard, Poli had been more successful than critics thought possible. By virtue of his attorney's influence and handiwork, Poli had more than 170 pieces of looted Huaca Rajada gold registered with the INC, making him their legal owner. However, he himself acknowledged that his "claim" might not be as solid as he first believed because each new administration debated the possible nationalization of all privately held pre-Columbian art collections.

Perhaps for this reason Poli had chosen to limit the number of tours of his collection, preferring to cater to foreigners. As Poli must have realized, any Peruvian he showed his collection to today might be the one who seized it for the government of Peru tomorrow.

Poli professed complete ignorance of the ongoing police investigations in Peru and the United States, and only mild curiosity as to why agents might be interested in how he had assembled his vast collection. He claimed not to know that seven of the remaining nine Huaca Rajada looters had been sentenced to jail time or probation, that Fred Drew had dropped from sight, or that Miguel Berckemeyer was wanted for questioning by police in the United States and Peru. Nor was Poli aware that his comments that afternoon would soon be part of a USIA report to the president of the United States, which would result, in June 1990, in stricter enforcement of antiquities regulations and a ban on the importation of all artifacts from Huaca Rajada.

No one besides Peruvian police knew how high up on the list of offenders of Peru's antiquities laws Poli was; but it was certain that, if Poli didn't head the list, his name was included on it. To the investigator's questions, Poli merely made a vague reference to a European museum tour of his Huaca Rajada treasures.

"I've been asked to be the principal exhibitor," he declared proudly, never once mentioning INC plans to exhibit more than five hundred restored pieces from the official collection in a separate tour.

Poli must have known how hard it might be to hold on to his precious booty, for just outside, across the street, two plainclothes officers sat in an unmarked police car, parked in the same place they had been for the past two weeks. Annoyed at their presence, Poli asked how long the police intended to harass him.

His visitor hadn't an answer. But in the mere asking of the question, Poli alluded to the truth about the change that had occurred in Peru since Ernil and his men had plundered Huaca Rajada. Poli's collection revealed more about its owner and his business practices than about the ancient past that his collection purported to glorify. Alva had known this all along, and now so did the police.

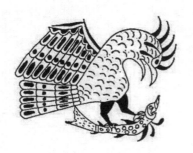

EPILOGUE

Walter Alva, director of the Bruning Museum, was awarded the "Order of the Sun," his nation's highest civilian or military honor, by President Alan Garcia in 1990. Despite repeated requests that Alva run for public office, he remains committed to his excavation at Huaca Rajada and to protecting the ancient monuments of Peru's north coast. In 2003 he inaugurated the opening of the Museum of the Royal Tombs of Sipan, which has since become a major tourist attraction in Sipan, Peru.

Miguel De Osma Berckemeyer is wanted for questioning by PIP investigators in Lima for his association with Fred Drew, and by United States Customs agents in connection with a shipment of antique furniture and pre-Columbian artifacts seized in Miami on October 23, 1988.

Charles Craig, retired Crocker Bank executive and Santa Barbara philanthropist, regained possession of all but 45 of the 398 artifacts removed from his Victorian town house on Arrellaga Street.

Christopher Donnan, professor of anthropology and director of the Fowler Art Museum at UCLA, assisted in the excavation of a royal Moche tomb at Moro, just south of Chiclayo, which contained the remains of a Moche high priestess. Between field seasons in Peru and his responsibilities at UCLA, Donnan organized the official touring museum exhibit of artifacts from Huaca Rajada, which made their United States debut in Los Angeles in October 1993.

Fred Drew is still keeping a low profile in Lima, pending criminal charges stemming from his involvement in the illegal export of pre-Columbian artifacts from Peru.

Murray Gell-Mann, Nobel Prize-winning physicist from Cal- Tech, returned his pre-Columbian art collection to Peru, and has published his autobiography, *The Quark and the Jaguar: Adventures in Simple and Complex*.

Alberto Jaime, the protester who caused Alva so much trouble in the first few months of his excavation, has become Huaca Rajada's official tour guide.

Benjamin Bishop Johnson, pioneer art conservator, died in his Santa Monica home on September 3, 1990, never having overcome the scandal that tainted his otherwise sterling career. He was fifty-two years old. Family members sold his vast antiquities collection, estimated to include more than 423 pre-Columbian artifacts, at Sotheby's on November 18, 1991.

Michael Kelly left the United States for Mexico soon after the conclusion of the civil lawsuit against Benjamin Johnson. Efforts to contact him there, or in London, have failed. According to Kelly's former associates, he is in Russia, where he hopes to coordinate a traveling exhibit of pre-Columbian artifacts.

Enrico Poli has stopped giving fifty-dollar tours of his art collection and resumed formal negotiations with INC officials in Lima to open the "Poli Pavilion of Peruvian Antiquities" in one of the two national museums.

George Roberts is currently trying to launch his own United States museum tour of Peruvian antiquities.

David Swetnam was released from the federal prison camp in Boron, California, in February 1990, and moved with his wife, Jacquelyn, and their hairless Peruvian dogs to Healdsburg, California, in the Sonoma Valley, and then to Seattle, Washington, where they remain active in the antiquities trade.

Edmundo Temoche took over the position of chief of police of Chiclayo upon the retirement of **Walter Mondragon** in 1988.

John Verano was awarded a research associateship at the National Museum of Natural History at the Smithsonian Institution in Washington, D.C., in 1989, where he is currently studying trepanation as practiced in prehistoric Peru.

Gaston Wallace, formerly a special agent for United States Customs stationed in Oxnard, California, has been promoted to division director of security operations in Washington, D.C. Like his former partner **Robert Casey**, he hails President George Bush's June 1990 ban on the importation of artifacts from Huaca Rajada.

Mercedes Zapata still lives in her home at Huaca Rajada, where she runs a concession stand to accommodate the needs of the five thousand or more visitors to the site each year.

Luis Chero Zurita never accepted his INC promotion to the rank of supervising archaeologist, but remains at Alva's side at Huaca Rajada and the Bruning. He and his wife, **Maria Fuentes**, and their two children live in a house nearby.

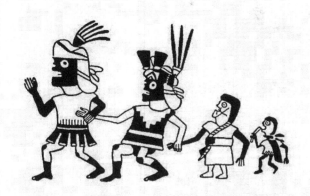

ACKNOWLEDGMENTS

My first debt is to Dr. Walter Alva, his wife, Susana Meneses, and their children, Bruno and Nacho, for their selfless support and help over the past three years. I benefited not only from their counsel but from their friendship as well.

Harvey Ginsberg, my editor at William Morrow, exhibited a kind heart and a keen eye for detail. His patience is matched only by that of agent Timothy Seldes, of Russell and Volkening.

For interviews, often supplemented by correspondence, my thanks go to Irving Azoff, Maximo Camacho, Robert Casey, Jaime Castio, Luis Chero Zurita, Brian Cook, Rosendo Dominguez, Christopher Donnan, Julio Galindo, Murray Gell-Mann, Benjamin Johnson, W. Noel Keyes, Augusto Lodi, Meryl Lori Macklin, Donna and Donald McClelland, Juan Martinez, Ronald Nessim, Tina Oldno, Enrico Poli, Trisha Reynales, George Roberts, Spurgeon Smith, George Stuart, David and Jacquelyn Swetnam, John Verano, James Vreeland, Adriana von Hagen, Gaston Wallace, Jr., and Mrs. Mercedes Zapata. Interviews with Juan Bernal, Fred Drew, and Michael Kelly were made available to me through intermediaries.

For help with translating, transportation, research, advice, criticism, or special insights, thanks must go to Brian Alexander, Miriam Altshuler, Jaime Arrieta, Joseph Broido, Tom Cook, Allana Cordy Collins, Kathryn Currey, Suzanne Du Pre, Donald Frederick, Sally Freitas, Julio Galindo, Joanne Hailey, Tom Hall, Andrew Havens, Anne Kalosh, Louisa Kam, Nancy Kelker, Jennifer Kirkpatrick, Katherine Kirkpatrick, Heinz Kohler, Vera Lentz, Daniel Levy, Stephen Lewin, Michael Long, Rosa Martin, William Moffett, Suzanne Muchnic, Marisa Nicely, Keith Praeger, Virginia Renner, Grosvie Robinson, Dennis Shimkoski, James F. Smith, Thelma Vickroy, Kim Walters, Lauri Weddell, Melanie Williams, George Wu, and the late Brian Borden.

Finally, special thanks must go to Guillermo Cock, an Andean scholar of the first rank, who first introduced me to Walter Alva, shot many of the photographs that appear in this book, and provided invaluable insights and suggestions through innumerable drafts of the manuscript. His wife, historian Mary Doyle, acted as my traveling companion and interpreter.

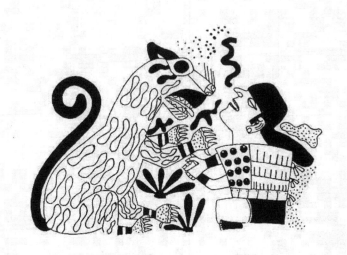

SOURCES
AND NOTES

Part 1: SEEDS FROM HEAVEN

February 6, 1987, the date I ascribe to the actual penetration of the first Huaca Rajada tomb, has been variously reported in newspapers and magazines as taking place as early as January 12, 1987, and as late as February 18. The primary reason for this profusion of dates is a confusion between the date when excavation began and the date when Ernil Bernal and his men made their first discovery.

A controversy also exists about whether Huaca Rajada was "generally believed" to have been a Moche site.

Before Ernil Bernal's discoveries, some archaeologists classified the site as Moche, although Alva and local townspeople considered the site to be Chimu.

In Chapter 2, I referred to Walter Alva as Dr. Walter Alva. From a strictly technical point of view, Alva does not have a doctoral degree recognized by an American university. Alva has, however, completed all the requirements for his doctorate, and would have had the official certificate in 1979 if a strike at the University of Trujillo hadn't prevented all doctoral candidates from receiving their degrees.

Police officials in Chiclayo arranged for me to tour the locations described in Chapters 2 and 4. They also furnished me with details of their investigation and subsequent raids. Susana Meneses and Walter Alva provided the key interviews for the material about Max Diaz in Chapter 3. Most of the other material in Chapter 3 comes from sources listed previously.

In deference to the wealth of research that archaeologists and other scholars have devoted to subjects that I touched on in Chapter 3, I think it is important for the reader to understand that very little is actually known about the history of huaquero activities on the north coast. Although no definitive proof exists to support my claim that the Incas looted their predecessors' temples, I have presumed this to be the case because of the vast quantities of gold and silver that the Inca removed from that area. Moreover, the Incas would not have looked favorably on Moche temples because of the well-documented Moche tradition of sodomy, a sexual practice that the Inca were known to have tried to abolish.

As described in Chapter 4, on January 26, 1990, Mercedes Zapata and her son Ricardo showed me their home and pointed out the locations of various tunnels that looters had carved into Huaca Rajada.

Enrico Poli provided the story recounted in Chapter 5 during an interview conducted on January 28, 1990. It should be noted, however, that though the artifact described at the end of Chapter 5 has been seen and photographed at the home of Fred Drew, he claims never to have left his home in Lima to purchase it.

A controversy exists over the gold figurine of the miniature lord described at the end of Chapter 5. Informed sources claim that Fred Drew never purchased this figurine, but that it was smuggled out of Peru by a third party and was recently sold to a collector in Switzerland for a reported $750,000. Equally informed sources claim that Fred Drew purchased this piece, turned it over to Berckemeyer, who in turn sent it to Swetnam, who sold it in England. Having seen photographs of the gold figurine that Drew purchased and the one purchased in Switzerland, I can say with some authority that the same Trujillo provider sold two similar gold figurines to two different customers. The provider didn't let his customers in on the secret because he wished to perpetuate the figurine's "one of a kind" status.

Part 2: HOUSE OF THE MOON

Material for Chapters 6 through 8 comes directly from inspections of the archaeological records held at the Bruning Museum in Lambayeque and interviews with Walter Alva, Luis Chero Zurita, Juan Brescia Lugon, and former Assistant Police Chief Edmundo Temoche.

While reading Chapter 6, the reader should keep in mind that before Huaca Rajada, no royal Moche tombs had ever been excavated. Assumptions Alva made about what a royal tomb looked like were based on examples of previously plundered tombs and burial platforms that he supposed had belonged to lords or Moche royalty.

A fascinating compilation of Lambayeque's myths and legends, many shedding light on the stories told by Mrs. Zapata, can be found in *Mitos, leyendas y tradiciones Lambayecanas*, written by Dr. Leon Barandiaran in 1921.

In Chapter 8, I relied heavily on *Panorama Mortal*, by Mabel Barreto, which I found to be one of the most complete and accurate published accounts of the shooting of Ernil Bernal. Additional information came from Chief of Police Temoche and Walter Alva.

Material for Chapter 9 comes from interviews that United States agents and reporters conducted with Fred Drew between January 1988 and August 1989, and correspondence between him and United States officials. At the time I sought to interview Mr. Drew in January 1990, he had gone into hiding and couldn't be reached. Any mistakes in this chapter are my own; however, every effort was made to corroborate all events with court records.

Miguel de Osma Berckemeyer, whose name both reporters and United States Customs agents have consistently misspelled, was also unavailable for an interview. Although he has publicly admitted his role in the smuggling operation, no formal charges or indictments have been brought against him.

Trisha Reynales, writing for *Conde Nast*, and Carl Nagin, reporting for PBS's Frontline and for *Art and Antiques* magazine, also contributed important background material for this chapter.

Part 3: TEMPLE OF THE FANGED DEITY

Interviews for Chapters 10 through 15 were conducted with Walter Alva, Luis Chero Zurita, Guillermo Cock, Christopher Donnan, and Juan Martinez between January and August 1990. As earlier, I also consulted the archaeological records and videotapes of the Huaca Rajada excavation on file at the Bruning Museum.

In Chapter 12, Christopher Donnan's comments about the plundered chambers at Huaca Rajada were mere speculation at this point. Tracing the precise moment when speculation ended and certainty began was hard, and I have arbitrarily done so here.

It is also important to note that Donnan uses the phrase "warrior-priest" to describe what Alva calls a "lord." Donnan also uses the phrase "presentation theme" to describe what Alva calls the "sacrifice ceremony." Although Donnan must be credited with first identifying the presentation theme and describing the central figure in that ceremony as a warrior-priest, I have chosen to use Alva's less cumbersome terms.

Material for Chapter 13 comes directly from the court records and testimony from United States v. David Swetnam, CR 88-00914, and Peru v. Johnson, CV 88-6990. Though David Swetnam was willing to confirm much of the information as presented, he chose to remain silent on two important points: smuggling techniques he used to bring the material in from Peru, and the names of his contacts at Peruvian customs.

Material for Chapter 17 comes directly from statements made by Michael Kelly, supported by documents seized at the home of Benjamin Johnson. Benjamin Johnson and his lawyer, Ronald Nessim, declined to comment on this particular incident.

Part 4: LORD OF SIPAN

Walter Alva's October 1988 article in *National Geographic* provided the outline and basis for Chapters 18 through 24. Also helpful were John Verano's prepublication article and both of Christopher Donnan's reports to the Research Committee of the National Geographic Society. Using these articles and unpublished reports as a foundation, I questioned Walter Alva, Luis Chero Zurita, Susana Meneses, Christopher Donnan, and John Verano to clarify any questions that I had.

As earlier, Chapters 21 and 25 relied heavily upon material from the criminal and civil court cases against David Swetnam and Ben Johnson. Gaston Wallace, interviewed in Washington, D.C., provided many insights and additional information for Chapter 21; his associate, Robert Casey, interviewed in Oxnard, provided similar assistance for Chapter 25.

In Chapter 21, the allegations about Michael Kelly were made by David Swetnam, not Customs agents. Then, as now, Customs held Michael Kelly to be a credible witness.

It is also important to note that David Swetnam has a different version of the events leading to the September 18, 1987, meeting between Kelly and Wallace. According to Swetnam, Kelly was using the threat of going to Customs to blackmail Swetnam into paying him a higher fee for helping to transport the artifacts. Swetnam refused to negotiate with him because he doubted Kelly would turn to Customs when only his name appeared on the paperwork. Swetnam also contends that Kelly was upset that Swetnam had obtained the exclusive services of Frank Thomas, a restoration specialist whom Kelly had arranged to come to America.

While Charles Craig declined to be interviewed for Chapter 25, I was able to corroborate almost all statements made about him through documents on file at the Santa Barbara Museum of Art, through Brian Cooke of Cookes Crating in Los Angeles, and by photos taken in the course of the raid at 21 W. Arrellaga Street in Santa Barbara. However, it should be noted that Mr. Craig's sworn affidavit differs from the account presented in this chapter in two significant ways. Mr. Craig claims that Customs agents asked to buy a pistol that they discovered in his bedroom. He also claims that an upstairs door was locked and later kicked open by Customs agents. Mention of these two alleged incidents were omitted from the text because they had little if any bearing on the antiquities investigation.

Part 5: HIGH PRIEST OF SIPAN

As earlier, articles and unpublished reports by Walter Alva, Christopher Donnan, and John Verano were instrumental in helping me to achieve a grasp of the material presented in Chapters 26, 27, and 28. Details about La Mina come directly from Walter Alva, Guillermo Cock, and Christopher Donnan.

Information about the ceramic dipper mentioned in Chapter 26 comes from Walter Alva and Luis Chero Zurita, not Christopher Donnan, who believes that the dipper cannot be used to explain the significance of this burial.

Spurgeon Smith, United States attorney for United States v. Swetnam, provided many of the key points for Chapter 29, as did George Roberts and Noel Keyes. Benjamin Johnson, whom I spoke to over the phone, initially expressed an interest in discussing the fine points of this case, but later referred me to his lawyer, Ronald Nessim. At best, Nessim provided only limited help, leaving me to rely on United States customs investigative records and court documents.

Part 6: OLD LORD OF SIPAN

Material for chapters 30 through 32 comes from on-the-site inspection by this author at Huaca Rajada, and interviews with Walter Alva, Luis Chero Zurita, Christopher Donnan, Nancy Kelker, Susana Meneses, Gaston Wallace, and John Verano.

In Chapter 30, allegations of a possible conflict of interest in George Roberts's handling of Peru v. Johnson never reached the press but were raised by Julio Galindo, the consul general of Peru.

George Roberts, Murray Gell-Mann, and Enrico Poli contributed to Chapter 33. Also helpful was the report of the Cultural Property Advisory Committee of the USIA, made available through Michael J. Kelly, chairman. Because of their ongoing investigation, the visitor to Poli's house has asked that his name not be used.